theatre & therapy

Theatre&
Series Editors: Jen Harvie and Dan Rebellato

Published
Susan Bennett: *Theatre & Museums*
Colette Conroy: *Theatre & the Body*
Jill Dolan: *Theatre & Sexuality*
Helen Freshwater: *Theatre & Audience*
Jen Harvie: *Theatre & the City*
Nadine Holdsworth: *Theatre & Nation*
Erin Hurley: *Theatre & Feeling*
Dominic Johnson: *Theatre & the Visual*
Joe Kelleher: *Theatre & Politics*
Ric Knowles: *Theatre & Interculturalism*
Caoimhe McAvinchey: *Theatre & Prison*
Bruce McConachie: *Theatre & Mind*
Helen Nicholson: *Theatre & Education*
Lionel Pilkington: *Theatre & Ireland*
Paul Rae: *Theatre & Human Rights*
Dan Rebellato: *Theatre & Globalization*
Trish Reid: *Theatre & Scotland*
Nicholas Ridout: *Theatre & Ethics*
Fintan Walsh: *Theatre & Therapy*

Forthcoming
Joel Anderson: *Theatre & Photography*
Lucy Nevitt: *Theatre & Violence*
Lourdes Orozco: *Theatre & Animals*
Juliet Rufford: *Theatre & Architecture*
Rebecca Schneider: *Theatre & History*
Harvey Young: *Theatre & Race*

Theatre& Series
Series Standing Order: ISBN 978–0–333–230–20327–3

You can receive future titles in this series as they are published by placing a standing order. Please contact your bookseller or, in case of difficulty, write to us at the address below with your name and address, the title of the series and the ISBN quoted above.

Customer Services Department, Macmillan Distribution Ltd
Houndmills, Basingstoke, Hampshire RG21 6XS, England

theatre & therapy

Fintan Walsh

palgrave
macmillan

First published 2013 by
PALGRAVE MACMILLAN

Palgrave Macmillan in the UK is an imprint of Macmillan Publishers Limited, registered in England, company number 785998, of Houndmills, Basingstoke, Hampshire RG21 6XS.

Palgrave Macmillan in the US is a division of St Martin's Press LLC, 175 Fifth Avenue, New York, NY 10010.

Palgrave Macmillan is the global academic imprint of the above companies and has companies and representatives throughout the world.

Palgrave® and Macmillan® are registered trademarks in the United States, the United Kingdom, Europe and other countries

ISBN: 978–0–230–29327–4 paperback

This book is printed on paper suitable for recycling and made from fully managed and sustained forest sources. Logging, pulping and manufacturing processes are expected to conform to the environmental regulations of the country of origin.

A catalogue record for this book is available from the British Library.

A catalog record for this book is available from the Library of Congress.

10 9 8 7 6 5 4 3 2 1
22 21 20 19 18 17 16 15 14 13

Printed in China

contents

series editors' preface

The theatre is everywhere, from entertainment districts to the fringes, from the rituals of government to the ceremony of the courtroom, from the spectacle of the sporting arena to the theatres of war. Across these many forms stretches a theatrical continuum through which cultures both assert and question themselves.

Theatre has been around for thousands of years, and the ways we study it have changed decisively. It's no longer enough to limit our attention to the canon of Western dramatic literature. Theatre has taken its place within a broad spectrum of performance, connecting it with the wider forces of ritual and revolt that thread through so many spheres of human culture. In turn, this has helped make connections across disciplines; over the past fifty years, theatre and performance have been deployed as key metaphors and practices with which to rethink gender, economics, war, language, the fine arts, culture and one's sense of self.

Theatre & is a long series of short books which hopes to capture the restless interdisciplinary energy of theatre and performance. Each book explores connections between theatre and some aspect of the wider world, asking how the theatre might illuminate the world and how the world might illuminate the theatre. Each book is written by a leading theatre scholar and represents the cutting edge of critical thinking in the discipline.

We have been mindful, however, that the philosophical and theoretical complexity of much contemporary academic writing can act as a barrier to a wider readership. A key aim for these books is that they should all be readable in one sitting by anyone with a curiosity about the subject. The books are challenging, pugnacious, visionary sometimes and, above all, clear. We hope you enjoy them.

Jen Harvie and Dan Rebellato

foreword

Between 1997 and 2008 I was a patient in what's generally called 'the mental health system'. During that time I collected phrases, 'gem-like' observations, that struck me as profoundly insightful and helpful. In 2005, as I gradually recovered and actively challenged the organisations, stigma and ignorance surrounding mental health, a clinical psychologist said to me,

> 'Mental illness, and its treatment, is a topic that
> provokes strong feelings, right across the board.'

It's my top phrase, these days, when questioned on issues of mental health.

In 1996, after a difficult year or two, I admitted to myself that I could no longer contain my mental anguish and despair, so I sought professional help. The following eleven years involved a long, often torturous, sometimes hilarious, mostly tedious trudge through mental illness and this 'mental health system' and the 'industry' surrounding it. Fortunately, in 2008, having finally got myself discharged from all mental health services, I emerged better – 'older and wiser' and more at peace with myself than ever before. And with a more sanguine view of the world and its ways.

So I know a lot about therapy, and a fair amount about theatre – and have plenty of strong feelings. Here are three stories taken from my experiences, relating to notions of theatre and therapy.

Story one

I trained as a painter at St Martin's School of Art between 1968 and 1972. When I left, I decided I would rather be a 'performance artist', as I couldn't see how my ideas would fit into the Fine Art 'gallery system'. After years of making all sorts of work in all sorts of settings I started to be asked to give talks about my work.

In about 1993 I performed *Drawing on a Mother's Experience* at an art school. Afterwards I gave a talk to a large group of students and staff. A young woman asked me this question:

'Is it therapy, your art?'

I felt aware of being in the 'hallowed halls of Fine Art' and so, somewhat emboldened by the enthusiastic reception of my show, where I had rolled around on the floor on a drawing made of food, I answered:

'Well all art is therapy, isn't it?'

There was a stunned silence, not even a titter, and two members of staff stood up and slowly walked out.

Story two

In 1997 I decided that a short spell at Pine Street Day Centre, a local state-funded 'therapeutic community' in London, would sort out my mental angst. I attended there, on and off, for a few years and learnt lots about people, society and mental health – my own and other people's.

When I was there I spent most of my time drawing in the art room, but there was endless group therapy, assorted activities, social events and so on. At one morning meeting we were told that a group of MA students who were training in drama therapy at Central School of Speech and Drama wanted to run a therapeutic drama group to get experience. Did anyone want to take part, the staff wondered? It wasn't my cup of tea and there was a fair amount of confusion about what would happen and what was expected of participants. But a few people signed up, and the weekly drama sessions started. I've no idea what happened as I didn't take part, but everyone dropped out after a couple of weeks. I felt sorry for the students, concerned for my friends, but mostly annoyed with the staff at the day centre, who hadn't done much to facilitate good communication and establish clear boundaries for all concerned.

A while later we got another invitation, to go to the Serpentine Gallery to take part in a one-day workshop run for 'people with mental health problems'. I decided to give it a try this time, mostly out of nosiness, and it sounded like a good day out. I had a great time; we all did, I think. We were shown round the exhibition before spending an afternoon in the Serpentine's posh art room working on collages – with tea and sandwiches as a cheering extra.

In the months following these two therapeutic interventions the impacts, or 'aftershocks', in the community at the day centre were strikingly different. There was a sense of loss, frustration and even gloom the first time round, compared with what felt like a buzzy breath of fresh air stirring us all towards new activities and increased self-respect.

Story three

In 2009 my family and I agreed that it was a good plan to exhibit a selection of the 711 diary drawings I had done during my somewhat lengthy journey through mental illness and beyond. The exhibition, *Bobby Baker's Diary Drawings: Mental Illness and Me, 1997–2008*, was shown at the Wellcome Collection in London for four months. It attracted an extraordinary number of people – over 50,000 – and a range of enthusiastic responses. I had the hunch that people might want to make comments after seeing the show. So we provided a Public book and a Private box for these reflections. Three big books were filled, and many, many cards.

A few months after the show I read all of them with my daughter Dora Whittuck, who co-curated the exhibition with me. It was very moving, with an immense range of responses. They were almost universally positive, except for one notable Public page that Dora drew to my attention. A group of drama and art therapists, who we assumed came as a group, had written a page of complaints that I hadn't credited these disciplines – of art and drama therapy – for making my drawings. They were clearly incensed to be left out. It hadn't occurred to them that I hadn't done the drawings in an art therapy group but had done them myself, on my own initiative. It was funny and strange that, as the trained professionals who surely must be the experts in this case, they felt collectively excluded from praise in this public arena of art and madness.

By sharing these short accounts of a variety of the strong feelings that I've encountered surrounding the arts, therapy and mental health, I hope to demonstrate diverse practices, perspectives and opportunities. My experience has led me to believe that starting with an open mind and striving for a degree of humility leads one on a fruitful quest towards knowledge and understanding of this valuable arena of the therapeutic role that the arts can play in our lives.

I'm particularly pleased therefore to read Fintan Walsh's book, which provides such an excellent account and context for this big subject, theatre and therapy.

Bobby Baker is a performance artist with a career spanning more than thirty-five years. She lives in London, UK, where her company Daily Life Ltd is based.

theatre & therapy

Theatre and the therapeutic tradition

Theatre, like therapy, can prompt us to reflect upon our own thoughts, feelings and behaviours in the presence of others, within a specific time frame. As we observe lives play out before us as spectators, or actively collaborate in the process as performers, practitioners and participants, theatre can illuminate and stimulate mental and emotional activity, those primary targets of therapeutic intervention. In the arousal of emotion, theatre can coax us to empathically identify with others. By stepping into another person's shoes, we might increase our sensitivity to others, and learn more about ourselves. Encounters with performance can deepen our awareness of behavioural patterns in a way that might even spur change. Theatre, like therapy, can lead us into a richer understanding of ourselves and our worldly relationships.

Those who work in theatre, or regularly frequent it, often claim that the experience can be transformative. In attempting to understand the way theatre might directly contribute to personal change, we can speak of its therapeutic *effect*. The victim of trauma who participates in one of Teya Sepinuck's Theatre of Witness projects only to develop a strong sense of insight and reconciliation might attest to this capacity, for instance. Many people claim that the charged nature of live performance can produce an intensity of thought and feeling whose impact is more subtle and resonant over time than it is immediately measureable. In considering this appeal, we might refer to theatre's therapeutic *affect*. The person who is moved during an intimate performance encounter with Adrian Howells knows theatre's potential to touch us in surprising and often inexplicable ways. Suffice to say it is also possible for theatre, like poorly practised therapy, to impact us in a range of negative ways, though this book is less concerned with such scenarios or outcomes.

As the examples listed in the previous paragraph suggest, we can think of theatre's therapeutic effects and affects in quite generous terms. Indeed, these days it is common to describe anything that makes us feel better, or is simply soothing, as therapeutic. However, it remains useful to have a clear sense of what we take the word 'therapy' to mean. Here, I primarily use the term to refer to the Western and particularly Freudian psychotherapeutic tradition invested in promoting mental and emotional well-being. (Of course, another book might be written on non-Western contexts or non-Freudian paradigms.) Professionally practised by psychiatrists, psychoanalysts, psychologists and counsellors, therapy usually involves a structured encounter between an individual, or a group, and a therapist. While conversation is the primary method used by most approaches, some therapies include movement, art-work and play. The word 'psychotherapy' combines the Greek words *psukhē* (meaning 'breath', 'spirit' or 'soul') and *therapeia* (meaning 'healing' or 'medical treatment'). As an interpretive tool for thinking about what some theatre and performance does, or strives to do, I take the term 'therapeutic' to encapsulate the aims, practices, effects and affects of work that engages purposefully with mental and emotional experience.

This book introduces readers to some of the fertile intersections between theatre and therapy, and analyses some of the historical, conceptual and practical points of contact between the disciplines. I argue that theatre and therapy share many connections, and suggest how a critical sense of 'the therapeutic' allows us to better understand what certain theatre and performance practices attempt to do. I write neither as a therapist nor as an advocate of the various types of therapy available; rather, I approach this topic as a theatre and performance researcher interested in points of overlap, difference and tension between the disciplines. Drawing on theatre from North America, the United Kingdom and Ireland, with reference to other contexts such as South America and Canada, my main argument is that theatre has been a source of inspiration for therapy since the latter's rise in the West in the late nineteenth century, and that theatre has mined, developed and extended this connection right up to the present day. Often I use the word 'theatre' to denote the performance event and all its components (which may include a dramatic text), and the word 'performance' to index the particularity of live encounters, acts or gestures. However, in seeing them as intrinsically and intricately linked within a broad spectrum of artistic activity, I often use the terms interchangeably.

To speak about the therapeutic dimension to theatre is to presume that therapy has a cultural as well as a clinical life. True enough, in the West at least, therapy has spread well beyond clinical settings. A case in point, HBO's hugely successful series *The Sopranos* (1999–2007) centres on mobster Tony Soprano's conversations with his therapist, Dr Jennifer Melfi, and more recently *In Treatment* (2008–2010) focuses on the patients of Dr Paul Weston, as well as his own personal life. While these television dramas exploit our obsession with therapy and use it as a device to expose character and relationships, there are plenty of less reflexive examples of mass therapy culture. Television talk shows from *Oprah* to *The Jeremy Kyle Show*, for example, spectacularise confession and cultivate public emotional discharge, while popular magazines such as *Psychologies* encourage us to anxiously and narcissistically sample our emotional states on a regular basis, while also supplying a language for this analysis. As Frank Furedi points out in *Therapy Culture: Cultivating Vulnerability in an Uncertain Age* (2004), this cultural pervasion does not simply benefit us, but generates and sustains the presumption that people are inevitably emotionally in trouble. As a profiteering industry, therapy culture is committed to producing a vast spectrum of neoliberal subjects who believe that there is always something wrong with their emotional lives, or that they are impossibly vulnerable to distress. For this reason, Furedi charges that, at worst, therapeutic culture is fundamentally invested in the 'management of subjectivity' (p. 22).

I do not seek to compound the trend Furedi highlights by subsuming theatre into a therapeutic discourse. Although I illuminate links between theatre and therapy, much of the work I examine (especially later in this section and in the last section) takes an interrogative position in relation to psychotherapy and therapy culture, often exploring its own therapeutic possibilities or limitations.

The four main sections of the book represent key points of contact between theatre and therapy. In examining these links, I am mindful not to dissolve the distinction between disciplines. To reduce them to mere equivalents would minimise the complexity and potential of both. Given the parameters of the series in which this book appears, I am aware that my study cannot be exhaustive. Instead, each section should be read as a critical snapshot that argues for particular ways of understanding the ties between theatre and therapy. Read cumulatively, the discrete sections will, I hope, provide a useful overview of the subject area, while possibly sparking new directions of thought, or signposting avenues for further inquiry.

This, the first section, surveys how drama and theatre captured the imaginations of the early pioneers of therapeutic theory and technique, many of whom looked to Greek and Shakespearian tragedies for inspiration. Here I also consider how this historical relationship has been represented in relatively recent theatre productions. The second section shifts focus from theatre production to examine approaches to actor training and audience engagement that have been shaped by therapeutic thought. In the third section I examine some deployments of drama and theatre strategies within therapeutic clinical settings. The final section is devoted to analysing the therapeutic dramaturgies and relations particular to a range of embodied, participatory contemporary theatre and performances practices, from the perspective of writers and theatre-makers, solo performers, audiences and communities. Here I suggest some of the ways contemporary theatre and performance can be seen to evolve neo-Aristotelian notions of catharsis, by centralising confession, physical and emotional intimacy, and richly affective encounters.

Therapists look to theatre

Most branches of therapy are indebted to the psychoanalytic thought of Sigmund Freud. Working in the late nineteenth and early twentieth centuries, the Austrian psychiatrist encouraged his patients to talk freely on his couch while he searched for primarily verbal cues to help understand their problems. Freud believed that the human mind operates at conscious and subconscious levels. He maintained that impulses repressed in the subconscious, which are not fully dealt with, inevitably create problems in our conscious, daily lives. Structured conversation, involving the analysis of dreams and fantasies, was the main method Freud developed in order to access his patients' hidden urges. Primarily,

Freud endeavoured to listen carefully to his patients in order to understand their difficulties. By enabling people to develop self-awareness through talking, Freud aimed to put them on the road to recovery.

In his writing, Freud frequently refers to dramatic texts or invokes theatrical metaphors to elaborate his thoughts on, and techniques for, what he describes as the 'science' of psychoanalysis as it advanced. In *The Interpretation of Dreams* (1899–1900; 1995) he refers to Sophocles' ancient dramatic tragedy *Oedipus Rex* (c.429 BC) to make observations on infantile sexuality, only to find in the Greek play a model for the psychoanalytic therapeutic practice that he was evolving at the time. Freud sees in Oedipus killing his father and marrying his own mother not only a representation of psychic organisation and familial desire, but also, in the slow, staged disclosure of this traumatic knowledge, an example of how the analytic process should proceed. 'The action of the play consists in nothing other than the process of revealing with cunning displays of ever-mounting excitement,' he writes, 'a process that can be likened to the work of a psycho-analysis' (p. 279).

Desire and emotion, conflict and trauma, concealment and disclosure: these are just some of the central preoccupations that connected drama and theatre to therapy in Freud's mind. And he did not stop discerning resonances at *Oedipus*. Many of Shakespeare's plays came under examination at various stages too, including *The Merchant of Venice* (c.1596), *Hamlet* (c.1600) and *Othello* (c.1603), to name a few.

In the paper 'Psychopathic Characters on the Stage' (1905–1906; 1942), Freud provides a detailed consideration of the similarity he perceives between theatre and therapy. He begins by alluding to Aristotle's view, as outlined in *Poetics* (*c*.335 BC), that the purpose of drama is to arouse 'terror and pity'. Identifying with characters on stage, Freud proposes, can 'purge the emotions' (p. 305). This processing of feeling, achieved by connecting with a character or dramatic narrative, is what Aristotle refers to as 'catharsis', translated from the Greek word *kathairein*, roughly meaning 'to cleanse' or 'to purify'. Some interpreters of Aristotle take the term to refer not only to the awakening of terror or pity, but quite generally to the cleansing of whatever is polluted within the tragic act, and possibly the spectator's own psychic life. Freud associates this phenomenon with the 'opening up of sources of pleasure or enjoyment in our emotional life', as takes place in joking, thinking or sexual excitement in everyday life. Essentially, we deal with our emotions by 'blowing off steam' (p. 305), and Freud suggests that the theatre can be a powerful outlet for this. It is worth pointing out that this theory has since been disputed as unrealistic by some psychologists and cognitive-behavioural therapists who believe that the way we deal with our emotions, insofar as they are connected to thoughts and behaviours, must be actively learned.

The adult audience member is not dissimilar to the child who plays, Freud maintains, to the extent that both imaginatively step into other people's shoes. With tragic drama, the spectator longs to be a hero and so he identifies with the character without putting himself in real physical danger. According to Freud, in the theatre the spectator can experience and process heightened emotions without significant risk, because he understands that someone other than himself is on stage, and it is only a game 'which can threaten no damage to his personal security' (p. 306). By engaging with the life represented on stage, the audience member can enjoy being a 'great man', can express 'suppressed impulses as a craving for freedom in religious, political, social and sexual matters' (p. 306). Although characters or performers may experience physical pain or danger, this can be a source of masochistic pleasure for the spectator, and ultimately relief, for he can identify with the situation without suffering bodily harm. In a reversal of expectations, Freud reveals how we actually enjoy observing other people's suffering. The continued relevance of this insight is perhaps best reflected in the widespread popularity of horror and disaster movies, Emergency Room television dramas and misery-laden soap operas.

While Freud distinguishes between the different kinds of struggles that underpin tragedies of character, social tragedies and religious drama, of greatest interest here is what he has to say about psychological drama. With this genre the battle is fought out in the protagonist's mind, 'a struggle between different impulses, and one which must have its end in the extinction, not of the hero, but of one of his impulses' (p. 308). Psychological drama turns into psychopathological drama when the source of the suffering is no longer a battle between two obvious forces, but a battle between a conscious urge and a repressed one. Neurotics will find this kind of drama enjoyable, Freud claims, while non-neurotics will meet it with aversion. We must remember that in Freudian thought to be neurotic is to be 'normal'. The neurotic has necessarily repressed passions through socialisation, while the non-neurotic has not. As we watch psychological drama unfold, Freud submits, our own repressed impulses can be awakened and 'worked through' – his term for coping with mental and emotional distress.

Freud believes that the first modern drama is *Hamlet*, insofar as it focuses on purposefully exposing the titular protagonist's neurosis. He writes that in the play we see a man 'in whom an impulse ... hitherto successfully repressed endeavours to make its way into action' (p. 309). Developing ideas described earlier in my discussion of *The Interpretation of Dreams*, Freud claims it is 'the dramatist's business to induce the same illness in us; and this can be best achieved if we are made to follow the development of the illness along with the sufferer' (p. 310). In creating a text for theatre, the dramatist must lower the audience's resistance so that we might enter into the neurotic life of the character – in this case Hamlet – and within that imaginary space deal with our own emotional quandaries. Some recent stagings of *Hamlet* radically foreground the play's psychological textures. For example, in Thomas Ostermeier's production for the Schaubühne, Berlin, which premiered in 2008, Hamlet (Lars Eidinger) is noticeably mentally dysfunctional, throwing himself on the clay-covered stage floor and wandering mischievously through the audience. In Ian Rickson's production for the

Young Vic, London, in 2011, Hamlet (Michael Sheen) is quite explicitly placed in a psychiatric unit.

A number of therapists working within the Freudian tradition have also looked to theatre to develop their theories and techniques. Writing in *The Tragic Effect: The Oedipus Complex in Tragedy* (1979), André Green conjectures that theatre can occupy a 'transitional position' between the individual and the social world. In the 'sentient, corporeal space' of performance we encounter things 'that both are and are not what they represent', he states. Theatre's 'tragic effect' relates to its ability not to expose the unconscious, but to carefully access it via a set of parallel substitutions on stage (p. 23). Within this model, the theatre is understood to construct a bridge between our public and private lives, our social and psychological selves.

French psychoanalyst Jacques Lacan, perhaps Freud's most eminent successor in the twentieth century, also devotes a substantial degree of attention to drama and theatre in his writings. However, while Freud often draws associations between art and the psychology of its maker, Lacan is more inclined to observe a distinction between the two. There is no direct relationship between the person and the art-object he or she makes, Lacan's work maintains. In other words, we cannot claim to know or understand Shakespeare's psychology just by reading or seeing *Hamlet*. This reasoning has much to do with Lacan's interest in post-structural linguistics, as largely developed by Swiss linguist Ferdinand de Saussure, which asserts that there is no direct connection between words and things.

Among Lacan's most sustained interpretations of drama are his readings of *Hamlet* and Sophocles' *Oedipus* and *Antigone* (*c.*441 BC). Examining these texts, Lacan maps tensions in the expression of desire through language. He posits that people, or subjects, move through various stages of consciousness in their lives, which roughly correspond to overlapping registers of meaning. These he terms the 'Real', 'Imaginary' and 'Symbolic' orders. The Real is before and outside language, the Imaginary is the domain of fantasy and the imagination, and the Symbolic is the realm shaped by language that mediates law, order and culture.

Leaving specific play references to one side for a moment, it is worth noting the sheer theatricality that underpins one of Lacan's most noted and influential essays, 'The Mirror Stage … ' (1949). Here he describes the child's perception of the 'spectacle' of his or her own image in a mirror at around six months old. This act – which might also be thought of as a process – events subjectivity in Lacan's schema. 'The *mirror stage* is a drama', he writes, 'that forces the child to realise that she is separate from her mother and divided within herself, and condemned to seek wholeness in the world of images for the rest of her life' (p. 5). For Lacan, this moment institutes for the child a sense of a private, psychic self at odds with a public, physical perception of self. From this moment on, humans continue to negotiate the relationship between these registers of understanding via encounters with others (through relationships or therapy, for example) and culture (through engagements with art and theatre, for instance). Of relevance here is not only how Lacan suggests we process our thoughts and feelings through representations, but the way he describes the birth of subjectivity as if it were a piece of theatre.

While many of the influential so-called post-Freudians do not give quite so much heed to theatre, the concept of play remains central, especially to those working with children. Austrian psychoanalyst Melanie Klein devotes considerable attention to play and fantasy in her work. Her 'object-relations' method focuses on interactions between the child and her environment, especially primary caregivers. Klein's play therapy techniques take into account how children's unconscious motivations are projected in play and drawing activities. For instance, in discussing her treatment of nine-year-old Grete in the paper 'Early Analysis' (1923), who she claims presents with 'strong homosexual fixations' (p. 101), Klein makes a direct link between theatre and sexual fantasy. She writes: 'theatre and concerts, in fact any performance where there is something to be seen or heard, always stand for parental coitus – listening and watching standing for observation in fact or phantasy – while the falling curtain stands for objects which hinder observations, such as bed clothes, the side of the bed, etc.' (pp. 101–2). Quite an extraordinary assertion by all accounts, Klein suggests that where children are concerned, fantasies of theatrical performance represent fantasies of parental sex.

Freud's daughter Anna also became a therapist, and developed a special interest in play and the psychoanalysis of children. However, while Klein believed that play itself could be used for analysis, Anna Freud adopted it as a strategy prior to in-depth treatment. In the latter's view, the process of playing allows children to adapt to reality, but it does not necessarily reveal their unconscious longings and battles.

British psychoanalyst Donald Woods Winnicott (D. W.), who studied under Klein, also celebrates play and interaction with transitional objects in child development. One of the most lucid writers of psychoanalytic thought, Winnicott believes that therapy is essentially a version of play. In *Playing and Reality* (1971) he writes: 'Psychotherapy has to do with two people playing together' (p. 51). Moreover, Winnicott claims that the aim of therapy might be to enable the client to free up his mental blockages by entering into play: 'where playing is not possible then the work done by the therapist is directed towards bringing the patient from a state of not being able to play into a state of being able to play' (p. 51). In a particularly colourful analogy contained in the paper 'The Capacity to Be Alone' (1958), Winnicott indicates that the positive experience of theatre can produce an 'ego orgasm' among spectators, and that this feeling might also occur through friendship, which he explains as the fruit of ego-relatedness, or more simply, intimacy and engagement (pp. 34–35). In the passage in question, sexuality, theatre and friendship form a curiously intimate alliance. The ideas of Winnicott continue to inform the use of drama and play for positive child development in educational settings.

Another important reference point here is US-born Christopher Bollas, who not only emphasises the value of art-work in child development, but also understands his patients in theatrical terms. In his book *Hysteria* (2000) Bollas describes how hysterical patients theatricalise themselves, 'transforming self into an event' (p. 117). 'Hysterical theatre is always something of a séance, as ghosts of the past are brought into some strange light and the hysteric feels himself or herself to be something of a medium for the transition of the absents into materialisation,' Bollas remarks. In therapy, patients invoke these characters from their personal lives, and in various ways perform them for the therapist to behold: 'There is true dramatic skill involved in the continuous evocation of parts of the mother, or parts of the father, or a brother, or a long since completed family event which only lives on in its theatrical rendering' (p. 126). Bollas' reading of the patient as a performer and the clinic as a theatre should not be taken as a simple rhetorical analogy. Rather, I think it usefully captures the fundamental performativity of expression and communication at the heart of theatre and therapy. It might be worth remembering what Bollas has to say about hysteria, theatre and haunting when we come to take a look at Daniel Day-Lewis' performance as Hamlet in the next section of the book.

While not all therapeutic models readily embrace psychoanalysis – indeed many contemporary branches identify with other psychological procedures entirely – most schools remain indebted to the Freudian tradition that centralises the unveiling of desires, conflicts and their negotiation in language. As has been revealed so far, among the most influential thinkers and practitioners of therapy – although the list above is by no means exhaustive – drama, theatre, performance and play are frequently invoked to develop and expand theories and techniques. Likewise, ideas in therapy have also come to help us understand drama, theatre and performance practice. When reading a text or observing a performance, we often find ourselves broaching questions of motivation, subtext, expression and feeling with a psychological lexicon to aid understanding. As Patrick Campbell observes of psychoanalysis and performance specifically in the introduction to *Psychoanalysis and Performance* (2001): 'In making the hidden visible, the latent manifest, in laying bare the interior landscape of the mind and its fears and desires through a range of signifying practices, psychoanalytic processes are endemic to the performing arts' (p. 1).

Naturalism and Surrealism

Although many examples of drama, theatre and performance throughout history are fecund grounds for the investigation of therapeutic ideas, Naturalism marks a more sustained commitment to exploring Freudian thought. While Naturalist theatre in the late nineteenth century was influenced by the evolutionary theories of Charles Darwin, the artistic movement both foreshadowed and was spurred on by developments in psychoanalysis. Foremost, Naturalist theatre was originally concerned with analysing the impact of heredity and environment on individuals, typically by examining character motivation.

French author Émile Zola is considered to be a pioneer of Naturalism in the theatre. In the essay 'Naturalism and the Theatre' (1881) Zola calls for a new style of theatre that would substitute 'physiological man for metaphysical man' (p. 765). The ideas of both Darwin and Freud informed Zola's contention that theatre needed to reflect humans under the influence of science and environment rather than gods, spirits and free agency, as had largely been the case until that time.

Swedish dramatist August Strindberg was one of Naturalism's most enthusiastic supporters in the theatre. Strindberg read Zola, who was keenly interested in what medicine was revealing about the human condition at the time. However, he was more drawn to Jean-Martin Charcot's and Hippolyte Bernheim's studies of hypnotism and suggestion, which also influenced Freud. (In the late nineteenth century, pioneering neurologist Charcot led weekly medical demonstrations of his 'hysterical' female patients in the Pitié-Salpêtrière Hospital, Paris, which Freud saw when he studied there in 1885. Patients were presented to those gathered in a staged, highly theatrical fashion, so much so that the line between theatre and therapeutic treatment was blurred even in these early days.) Strindberg's fascination with latent impulses, torturous desire, culture and genetics was channelled into some of his most vivid plays, including *The Father* (1887), *Miss Julie* (1888) and *Creditors* (1889). While Naturalist artists frequently frowned upon the Romantics who had preceded them, Strindberg appealed to this earlier tradition, and its influence can be discerned in the intensity of emotions that his plays chart.

Many scholars claim that Strindberg largely preceded Freud. However, it seems likely that Strindberg's

A Dream Play (1901) was at least coloured if not shaped by Freud's work, given that it was written the year after *The Interpretation of Dreams* was published. As protagonist Agnes descends to Earth to observe the plight of humankind in this play, scenes flow into and out of one another, and highly symbolic imagery abounds. Between 1892 and 1897 Strindberg experienced severe mental problems, which are documented in his autobiographical novel *Inferno* (1898). *A Dream Play* was composed shortly after this period, and he refers to it in his letters to Emil Schering as his 'best loved Play, the child of my greatest pain' (*Strindberg's Letters*, 1992, p. 738). The drama might well be perceived as a working-through of the artist's personal turmoil, as well as a representation of that suffering. In the foreword to the text Strindberg writes of his intention:

> In this dream play, the author has ... attempted to imitate the inconsequent yet transparently logi-cal shape of a dream. Everything can happen, everything is possible and probable. The charac-ters split, double, multiply, evaporate, condense, disperse, assemble. But one consciousness rules over them all, that of the dreamer; for him there are no secrets, no scruples, no laws. (*Miss Julie and Other Plays*, 1998, p. 176)

The play's emphasis on fluid form and a layered landscape, as reflected in this quotation, can be seen to mirror the complex, dynamic psychic topography mapped by Freud.

A Dream Play also represents a bridge between Naturalism and Surrealism. The Surrealists were more directly influenced by Freudian thought, and encouraged the use of the psychoanalytic techniques of free association, dream analysis and unconscious recovery in their artistic practice. Developing out of the Dada movement, and thriving after World War I, Surrealism can also be interpreted as a visceral reaction and antidote to the rationalism deemed by many to be responsible for war in the first place. Surrealism was more interested in sense and feeling than logical understanding. Writing in the 'Surrealist Manifesto' (1924), Surrealist pioneer and French artist André Breton condemns what he saw as the then prevalent 'realistic' attitude. Associating it with positivism, Breton declares that it is 'hostile to any intellectual or moral advancement'. Championing the discoveries of Freud, Breton proposes that artists should mine their psyches for inspiration:

> The imagination is perhaps on the point of reasserting itself, of reclaiming its rights. If the depths of our mind contain within it strange forces capable of augmenting those on the surface, or of waging a victorious battle against them, there is every reason to seize them – first to seize them, then, if need be, to submit them to the control of our reason.

In Breton's assertion we see how reason was understood to produce internal repression and external violence.

The Surrealists hoped that the exploration of psychic life might lead to greater personal, interpersonal and cultural understanding.

Paris was a hub of Surrealist activity in the early twentieth century, and Alfred Jarry emerged as an important figure in the world of theatre. His play *Ubu Roi* (1896) satirises authority by emphasising carnality, the grotesque and bodily excess on stage, and in doing so it can be viewed as anticipating some of the Surrealist theatre experiments of the 1920s and 1930s. However, Antonin Artaud, later termed an 'Absurd' artist by Martin Esslin, became the most noted and influential figure in Surrealist theatre at this time. Artaud was appointed director of Paris' Bureau of Surrealist Research in 1924, although he was dismissed from the position two years later. With Roger Vitrac and Robert Aron, he set up the Théâtre Alfred Jarry in Paris in 1926, which staged Surrealist theatre for two seasons, including Strindberg's *A Dream Play*. For most of the 1930s he wrote essays and manifestos. Like Strindberg, Artaud suffered numerous psychotic breakdowns, and was even treated by a young Lacan at one point. Declared insane in 1937, he was hospitalised for most of the remainder of his life until he died in 1948.

In his writings on what he referred to as Theatre of Cruelty, published in *The Theatre and Its Double* (1938), Artaud rails against the 'agonized poetry' expressed in theatres' 'bizarre corruptions' (p. 9), which ought instead to be outlets for venting our repressions. While European culture historically celebrated mind over body, words over feeling, Artaud champions a 'culture of force and exaltation' (p. 10) to demolish this restrictive rationalism. In the spirit of Freudian thought, Artaud proffers that everything 'has a shadow which is its double' (p. 12), and claims that theatre ought to invest in 'naming and directing shadows' (p. 12).

Artaud calls for a kind of theatre that would restore 'a passionate and convulsive conception of life' (p. 122). However, whereas Freud and his successors explore ways to carefully peel back the layers of their clients' egos and unlock repressed impulses, Artaud aims to jolt spectators into enlightenment through visual, physical and affective force. Language socialises and thus represses us, in Artaud's view, and so he imagines a theatre that would disrupt this bind. Mirroring Bertolt Brecht's condemnation of 'culinary theatre', Artaud describes the work around him as 'digestive theatre' – light entertainment – that pays little attention to psychological sensitivity. In place of this, Artaud conceives of a theatre that plays on the nerves and senses by centralising visual and physical intensities, vibrations and dissonances (p. 125).

Despite its affinities with aspects of Freudian thought, Artaud's Theatre of Cruelty is not invested in talking cures, or the careful guiding of its audience to self-knowledge. Rather than offering a system of actor training, Artaud supplies a poetic vision of a theatre disinterested in character, narrative or logic, whose primary aim is to produce psychic and bodily affects that might shock spectators into heightened awareness or insight. This would be the stimulus for a kind of cleansing and transformation, different from Aristotelian catharsis insofar as it is not premised upon a process of spectatorial identification with character or action. Given his challenge to logocentrism and rationality, Artaud later became an important reference point in the writings of two French psychoanalysts and intellectuals who were highly critical of ego-based psychoanalysis and Oedipal hierarchies, namely Gilles Deleuze and Félix Guattari. In *What Is Philosophy?* (1994), admiring Artaud's ambitions, they write: 'Artaud said: to write for the illiterate – to speak for the aphasic, to think for the acephalous' (p. 109). Throughout the twentieth century, Artaud's writings were a touchstone for anyone interested in developing or interpreting highly visual, physical or affective art practices, some of which we will look at in the final section. In particular, his writings were the inspiration behind Julian Beck and Judith Malina's Living Theatre (1947–). Artaud's ideas also informed the work of performance and body artists active from the 1960s onwards, such as the Viennese Aktionists, who treated subjectivity and identity as inextricable from the social and political shaping of the body.

Theatre about therapy

While the Oedipal narrative both informs and is interrogated by many plays in Western theatre throughout the twentieth century, often through explorations of sexual desire and its policing (from the hothouses of Tennessee Williams' drama to the metatheatrical landscapes of Caryl Churchill's theatre), a number of dramas written and produced in the latter half of the century specifically address figures and moments within the therapeutic tradition. Many of these works strive to understand the private lives of therapy's pioneers, its politics and its legacy, including the on-going relationship between theatre and therapy.

French feminist literary critic and author Hélène Cixous has written a number of plays broaching psychoanalytic and theatrical subjects, such as *Portrait of Dora* (1976) and *The Name of Oedipus: Song of the Forbidden Body* (1978). In the former, Cixous rewrites one of Freud's most detailed and contentious case studies from a feminist perspective. In *Fragment of an Analysis of a Case of Hysteria* (1901; 1905), Freud charts his treatment of Ida Bauer, referred to as Dora, who presents with the symptom of aphonia, or loss of voice. While Freud considers his analysis to be somewhat incomplete, he makes a diagnosis of hysteria on the basis of two dreams he deems to be significant. However, many feminist critics have since taken issue with Freud's presumption of passivity among his female patients.

First staged by Simone Benmussa in 1976, Cixous' play takes Dora's case and reconstructs it by nuancing Freud's published evaluations and centralising Dora more in her own story. Dora recounts her dreams and experiences for the audience in the present, while remembered scenes are enacted around her. Whereas Freud dismisses Dora's attachments to Mrs K. and her mother, seeing them as marginal presences or even signs of weakness, Cixous underscores Dora's relationships with women, and associates them with her strength. Crucially, Cixous deploys the theatrical form to displace Freud from his own case study.

Although in the dramatic text Cixous indicates that Freud's study room should be represented, he himself is effectively removed from this retelling, and Dora speaks to us for herself. As she addresses the audience, we unwittingly take on the role of analyst, and are prompted to ask questions ourselves about the construction and retelling of personal and subjective experience. In Cixous' play, not only are Freud's findings challenged, but the theatre itself is presented as something of an analytic space for disclosure, remembrance and reimagining.

Terry Johnson's *Hysteria: Or Fragments of an Analysis of an Obsessional Neurosis* premiered at the Royal Court, London, in 1993, directed by Phyllida Lloyd. Set in 1938, it concentrates on the final year of Freud's life as he suffers from cancer, when he was living at 20 Maresfield Gardens, Hampstead. Johnson's play centres on the dramatic elaboration of Freud's real-life meetings with Salvador Dalí and the Jewish historian Professor Yahuda, who asked him not to publish his iconoclastic study *Moses and Monotheism* (1939) at a fraught time for the Jewish people.

While Johnson's play takes two actual meetings as a stimulus, he gives us a fantastical rather than a biographical study. A core stimulus for the farcical comedy is Jessica, a young female character who appears from behind French windows. The daughter of a patient Freud cured of hysterical paralysis thirty years prior to this meeting, she has some tough questions to ask the therapist about his work, mocking penis envy and the idea that he knew anything about comedy. In pursuing a farcical mode, Johnson's play implodes some of the tensions that surround Freud's legacy, in particular his conflation of hysteria and passivity with women.

Another play taking a biographical angle is Nicholas Wright's *Mrs Klein*, which is based on the life of Melanie Klein. It premiered at the National Theatre, London, in 1988 under Peter Gill's direction, and has been staged a number of times since, including an acclaimed revival at the Almeida, London, in 2009, directed by Thea Sharrock. In the play, which is set in London in 1934, Klein is both admired and condemned for her insights on childhood. However, her relationship with her own daughter Melitta, who is also a psychoanalyst, is in disarray. As Klein departs for Budapest to attend the funeral of her son, a mysterious refugee named Paula steps in to manage her life. Klein's daughter arrives to reveal that her brother killed himself, and when her mother comes home, their family secrets and gripes are aired.

As with Johnson's drama, Wright's play builds upon the fascination that people seem to have with therapists' private lives. Part of this allure, I suspect, arises from a tendency to think that if therapists' lives are messed up, we are not doing so badly ourselves. Although Klein wrote extensively on raising children, the play exposes her own difficulty in parenting. While this angle manages to personalise and historicise Klein's work, it also allows the audience to assume the role of analyst of her life. Further, as with the effect of watching the heroes of tragedy which Freud wrote about, and I discussed earlier, in observing the private toils of the 'heroes' of therapy, we might also feel better about our personal challenges and shortcomings.

Glasgow-based theatre company Suspect Culture explored the interface of contemporary psychoanalysis and experimental performance in its production *The Escapologist* (2006). This piece takes as its starting point the essayist and psychoanalytic psychotherapist Adam Phillips' book *Houdini's Box: On the Arts of Escape* (2001). In this text, Phillips juxtaposes case studies of people who came to his clinic with histories of trying to escape relationships, commitments or consequences with analyses of the world's most famous escape artist, Harry Houdini. One way of discovering what a person wants, Phillips exhorts, is to find out what he is trying to get away from. Phillips reasons that in performing with the symbolic props of beds, jails, skyscrapers and trunks, Houdini not only demonstrated how 'the body might be tested, or endangered, or exploited, or confined' (p. 88), but performed the fantasies of escape particular to his time.

Written by Simon Bent, and originally directed by Graham Eatough, Suspect Culture's show has at its heart a psychotherapist who mines the desires of his patients: a doctor struggling to cope with her father's death, a builder trying to cope with his wife's departure, and a young girl failing to accept her mother's new relationship. Doubting the credibility and efficacy of his own work, the therapist is drawn to the life of Houdini, who, as Phillips writes, turned 'scepticism into a performance art' (p. 15). As in Phillips' assessment of escape artists, who always need something new to flee from, the characters in this play find it easier to pursue flights of fancy and adventure than face the truth about themselves. The opening scene perhaps best captures the theatricality of the escapist's psychology and the therapeutic scenario which Phillips writes about: a straitjacketed man dangles by his ankles from a chain, Houdini-like. Lowered to the ground, he wriggles free, before taking his place on the therapist's couch.

Although it does not deal with a key figure in the history of therapy, Anthony Neilson's *The Wonderful World of Dissocia* explores the subjective experience of mental illness, as well as attitudes towards it and its treatment in contemporary culture. First developed with students at LAMDA in 2002, the play was later revised and produced by the National Theatre of Scotland in 2004. It follows what is essentially an *Alice in Wonderland* structure: in the first act, the protagonist Lisa encounters a range of bizarre characters in the fantastical land called Dissocia, which is ostensibly a depiction of her delusional imaginings; and in the shorter second section we see Lisa in a hospital bed being tended to by her family and doctors. One of the questions Neilson's play seems to ask is what is lost in therapeutic intervention, particularly medical treatment? It does so by showing us two perspectives on psychic life: one in which the ostensibly 'troubled' mind gives us access to limitless perceptions and experiences, and one in which that mind is something to be disciplined, controlled and effectively rendered inert.

Similar questions permeate Sarah Kane's dramatic corpus. While much has been said about the fact that Kane experienced depression and ultimately committed suicide in 1999, her writing is incredibly rich in its exploration of the relationship between mental illness, theatre and therapy. This is especially true of *4.48 Psychosis*, which is the last play Kane wrote, in the months before her death. Although three actors delivered the text when it was first performed at the Royal Court, London, in 2000, the play itself does not designate character. Instead, the drama reads like the scored, fragmented thoughts of what seems to be one mind suffering extreme mental disorientation and distress. The voice refers to a range of interpersonal, therapeutic and medical interventions striving to offer relief, none of which really work. 'Dr This and Dr That and Dr Whatsit' (p. 209) are largely ineffective and primarily humiliate the subject. And at 4.48 a.m., everything is at its most terrifying:

> At 4.48
> when depression visits
> I shall hang myself
> to the sound of my lover's breathing. (p. 207)

In exquisitely wrought language, Kane offers us rich insight into the experience of mental suffering. Further, she seems to connect the experience of both making and experiencing theatre as one way in which we might develop insight into and relief from emotional or psychic turmoil. Optimistically, the closing line, 'please open the curtains' (p. 245), can be taken as an invitation to explore our mental and emotional lives through participating in the theatre as makers or spectators.

So far we have looked at certain historical ties between theatre and therapy. I have charted some of the ways pioneering therapists looked to drama, theatre, performance and play to develop their theories and techniques. In Naturalism and Surrealism, Freudian thought inflected drama and theatre practice. We have also seen how, in the latter half of the twentieth century, writers and theatre-makers reveal a fascination with this historical bind between disciplines, although they frequently seem to posit theatre as an equally powerful vehicle in the analysis of analysts and human behaviour. Shifting perspective slightly, we will continue to discover how certain psychological perspectives have informed approaches to actor training and audience engagement.

Actor training and audience engagement

On 5 September 1989, while playing the title role in Richard Eyre's production of *Hamlet* for the National Theatre, London, Daniel Day-Lewis walked off stage and did not return. As the ghost of Hamlet's father appeared to him, Day-Lewis is reported to have sobbed uncontrollably before leaving the stage. While newspapers speculated that the then thirty-two-year-old actor had suffered a break-down, and Eyre documented in his diaries that Day-Lewis had encountered difficulties with the space, the play and 'an excess of ambition' (*National Service: Diary of a Decade at the National Theatre*, 2003, p. 84), the actor eventually claimed that he had experienced a vision of his own father on stage, the former poet laureate Cecil Day-Lewis, who had died seventeen years earlier. Interviewed by Simon Hattenstone for *The Guardian* in 2003, Day-Lewis recalls: 'I had a very vivid, almost hallucinatory moment in which I was engaged in a dialogue with my father ... yes, but that wasn't the reason I had to leave the stage. I had to leave the stage because I was an empty vessel' (28 February 2003). Playing Hamlet encounter his dead father, Day-Lewis found himself speaking to his own.

Whatever actually happened to Day-Lewis on the night in question, his description of being overcome by another presence or reality is especially provocative for beginning to think about actors' emotional investments in roles. *Hamlet* is a play about many things, not least of all the relationship between a son and his father, and the process of grieving. In *The Interpretation of Dreams*, Freud sees the drama as being concerned with bereavement on a number of levels. Mourning is not just particular to Hamlet, according to Freud: on the basis of certain autobiographical reports, it can also be seen to relate to a reputed personal loss of Shakespeare's:

> I observe in a book on Shakespeare by Georg Brandes (1896) a statement that *Hamlet* was written immediately after the death of Shakespeare's father (in 1601), that is, under the immediate impact of his bereavement and, as we may well assume, while his childhood feelings about his father had been freshly revived. It is known, too,

that Shakespeare's own son who died at an early age bore the name of 'Hamnet,' which is identical with 'Hamlet.' (p. 283)

Suffice to say, there are numerous hauntings at work in Shakespeare's play. It is for this reason that in his book *The Haunted Stage: Theatre as Memory Machine* (2003), Marvin Carlson refers to it as 'the most haunted of all Western dramas' (p. 4), with the role of Hamlet conjuring the 'most crowded field of ghosts' (p. 81).

'Haunting' is an especially evocative way to describe the work of theatre. Figures appear and disappear, moving us before moving on. In live performance, memories of the theatre, the play, actors, friends, enemies, and numerous associations besides, are conjured in the present, so that we are rarely without some kind of spectral presence. Herbert Blau, a scholar interested in the intersection of psychoanalysis and performance, writes of theatre's essential ghostliness in *The Audience* (1990): 'Theater is made from this play of meaning in a structure of becoming, the passing form of an invisible force, where we lose meaning by finding it, and there is always something repressed' (p. 57). As Day-Lewis' experience reveals, actors are also susceptible to a range of hauntings. While bearing in mind the various competing interpretations of this rather extreme incident, I suggest that one of the things we might surmise is that the performer became so immersed in his character that he virtually lost all sense of self.

Day-Lewis is often acclaimed and sometimes ridiculed for his meticulous preparation of roles. He identifies with his characters to such an extent that he spends a lot of time off stage or screen in role. In playing the part of Christy Brown, who had cerebral palsy, in the film *My Left Foot* (1989), for example, Day-Lewis stayed in a wheelchair for most of his time on set, and was spoon-fed by the crew. In preparing for Bill the Butcher in Martin Scorsese's *Gangs of New York* (2002), Day-Lewis trained as a butcher, and claims to have wandered in character through the streets of Rome, where the movie was filmed, picking fights.

This process of building character draws upon the Method approach to acting. This style is rooted in Russian director Constantin Stanislavski's system of actor training, as developed in America by Lee Strasberg. Stanislavski is a seminal figure in directing actors to focus on personal psychology and emotional motivation in the preparation of roles. It is in Stanislavski's so-called System that we first see a sustained focus on the performer's interior life, rather than just his physical apparatus. In his first book on acting, the instructive novel or mock diary *An Actor Prepares* (1937), Stanislavski claims that the performer should 'study the life and psychology of the people who surround him ... An actor creates not only the life of his times but that of the past and future as well. That is why he needs to observe, to conjecture, to experience, to be carried away with emotion' (p. 208). Consistent with this approach, Stanislavski's 'psycho-technique' requires actors to mine their emotional memories in order to identify with and build their characters. They must awaken their subconscious impulses via the creative process: 'the fundamental objective of our psycho-technique is to put us in a creative state in which our subconscious will function naturally' (p. 303). While Stanislavski did not initially describe technical methods for unleashing the subconscious, he impresses on us how the actor's emotional register will change: '*Beforehand* we have "true-seeming feelings", *afterwards* — "sincerity of emotions"' (p. 304).

While Stanislavski promoted the use of emotional memory at the First Studio of the Moscow Art Theatre, which he founded in 1912 to train actors, he also realised that some performers were susceptible to losing control. This was the case with his protégé Michael Chekhov, who had a breakdown when he experimented with emotional memory, later rejecting its centrality in the development of his own actor training practice. To alleviate this danger, Stanislavski began using more reliable ways of accessing emotion, focusing on the actor's imagination rather than personal memory. This shift led to his development of the Method of Physical Actions, which relied upon physical gestures to trigger emotions.

Despite a shared interest in awakening subconscious impulses, there is little evidence to conclude that Stanislavski was directly influenced by Freud, whose work was translated into Russian in 1910. Rather, as noted in *An Actor Prepares*, he was inspired by the French psychologist Théodule-Armand Ribot, who developed the concept of 'affective memory' in his work. However, in the evolution of his System in America as Method acting, stronger Freudian influences were at play, to the extent that actor training sometimes resembled actor therapy.

Method acting was first popularised in the US by the Group Theatre in New York City in the 1930s, and it was subsequently developed by Lee Strasberg at the Actors Studio from the 1940s until his death in 1982. In the 1930s, Freudian psychoanalysis flourished in America, and it directly influenced Method training. Along with Carl Jung, Freud delivered his first and only series of lectures in the US at New York's Clark University in 1909, and was much more warmly received than he had been in Europe. According to Jonathan Pitches in *Science and the Stanislavsky Tradition of Acting* (2006), the first mention of psychoanalysis on stage in New York City can be dated to 1912, and Freud was explicitly referenced in Clare Kummer's farcical comedy *Good Gracious, Annabelle*, which played at the Republic Theatre, New York, in 1916 (p. 96).

Some of the most famous Method performers involved in the early days of the Actors Studio attended analysis. For example, Elia Kazan, Montgomery Clift and Marlon Brando all entered therapy. Marilyn Monroe, who read Freud, entered analysis upon the recommendation of Strasberg. Her many therapists included Anna Freud (to whom she left some of her estate) and Marianne Kris, who lived in the same apartment block as Strasberg in New York.

Alongside Freudian psychoanalysis, the behavioural psychology of figures such as Aleksei Gastev and John Broadus Watson gained popularity in America. Whereas Freudian thought focused on the analysis of subjective, interior experience, behaviouralism was more concerned with objective, external action. Both strands contributed to the tuning of Stanislavski's System in the work of Richard Boleslavsky, who is largely responsible for introducing it to the US, and of teachers Stella Adler and Sanford Meisner. But out of these, it was Strasberg who experimented most with the Freudian schema.

Strasberg read Freud, and his advancement of Stanislavski's ideas was greatly influenced by this experience. Actors were advised to enter analysis, and encouraged to appeal to unconscious experience in training and preparing roles. In dealing with actors, Strasberg stresses the importance of relaxation, concentration and affective memory. In his writings, he often describes assuming the role of therapist to solicit a better performance from his students.

In his book *A Dream of Passion: The Development of the Method* (1987), Strasberg gives us a sense of how his approach worked. Describing a female actor who complains of a pain in her neck, Strasberg seeks out a psychological cause in her youth. He solicits that as a child she had to share a bed with her sister, who threatened to kill her if she did not lie still. Strasberg labels this incident 'traumatic', and deems the experience to be responsible for the actor's neurosis, which he understands to manifest as a physical symptom. His intervention aims to release the 'mannerisms and tension that interfered with her ability to express herself on stage' (p. 97). For Strasberg, talk and relaxation reduced mental and emotional tension, which in turn had physical effects: 'The area had to be approached through the connection between mind and body, a major aspect of most schools of modern psychology' (p. 99). Actor Richard Durham, who took classes with Strasberg in the 1950s, describes his teacher's approach to affective memory in terms that evoke a quasi-therapeutic encounter: actors would sit in chairs, relaxed, while Strasberg would lead them into a 'dream-like sensory journey into a incident in the actor's past experience' (cited in Pitches, p. 116).

While numerous approaches to actor training throughout the twentieth century centralise the performer's psychology in creating and portraying a role, and indeed connecting with the audience, many methods either foreground physical processes or consider them alongside emotional impulses.

This is the case with Vsevolod Meyerhold's biomechanics, Michael Chekhov's psychological gesture and Jerzy Grotowski's and Phillip Zarrilli's psychophysical acting. For the latter two, and perhaps particularly for Grotowksi, spiritualist thought and practice is also formative. Even though Stanislavski championed physical actions later in his career, in Method acting the focus on analysing interior life almost resembled a therapeutic procedure in its own right, where self-reflection was understood to produce a better performance. In *The Player's Passion: Studies in the Science of Acting* (1993), Joseph Roach reminds us that debates surrounding the relationship between the mind and the body have always been less abstract and more immediate to performers: 'The central issues of psychology and physiology, by whatever names they are known, are not remote abstractions to the performer, but literally matters of flesh and blood' (p. 16). While a range of approaches to actor training continued to explore this contentious dualism throughout the twentieth century, the embodied nature and impact of performance were also routinely tested in the use of drama and theatre strategies within therapeutic contexts.

Drama and theatre in therapy

Most civilisations and societies have believed in the healing potential of the expressive arts, including creative participation and forms of ritual enactment. In the first section of this book, for example, we saw how Aristotle perceived ancient Greek theatre to have a cathartic function, long before therapy became formally organised. This section reviews some of the ways in which drama and theatre have been formally harnessed within therapeutic contexts over time, looking at a selection of medical, psychological, educational and socially engaged interventions.

Taking issue with the established medical procedures of his day, the Ephesian physician Soranus, who practised in Rome in the second century AD, believed that mentally ill patients should be put in calm surroundings where they could read, talk and participate in theatre productions. In the fifth century AD, Caelius Aurelianus advocated that people suffering from madness should attend the theatre. In terms of early dramatic representation, Shakespeare's plays include rich and provocative representations of madness, and in some cases even imply how theatre might intervene: the play within the play in *Hamlet*, for example, is used to produce clarity within the court of Elsinore, and in *King Lear*, Edgar

uses what might now be described as a form of dramatic vis-
ualisation to assist his father, Gloucester. In some so-called
lunatic asylums during the seventeenth and eighteenth centuries, theatre was used as part of treatment. For example,
as early as 1813, theatres were constructed in hospitals at
Aversa, Naples and Palermo, Italy. However, by the start of
the twentieth century, with advances in psychological disciplines, we see a more sustained investigation into the therapeutic value and potential of drama and theatre practices.

Stanislavski, discussed in the previous section, was by no
means the only theatrical innovator to emerge from Russia
at this time. Contemporary Nikolai Evreinov, who knew
Stanislavski's work, also made important contributions in
his plays and critical writings, particularly in proposing
the theatricality of everyday life and advocating the use of
theatre as a therapeutic medium. Evreinov was significant
in the development of monodrama, which in its emphasis
on externalising an individual's psychic life, in many ways
anticipated the monologue drama that we will look at in the
final section of this book. Between 1915 and 1924, Evreinov
produced a series of monographs and pamphlets outlining
his theories, and he was director of the Distorting Mirror
Theatre, St Petersburg, from 1910 to 1917.

In *The Theatre in Life* (1927), Evreinov elaborates most thor-
oughly on the therapeutic power of theatre, or what he refers to
as 'theatrotherapy'. In developing this concept, he recommends
theatre as therapy for actors and audiences, theatre as an instinct,
theatre and play as vital for intellectual development, and the
stage management of life. 'The theatre cures the actors. It also

cures the audience' (p. 126), Evreinov argues, while conceding that '[t]heatrotherapy is still in its initial stage of development' (p. 127). Evreinov maintains that simply framing experience as theatre can create a 'theatre for oneself'. While he affirms that theatre is thus everywhere, and necessary for the health of humankind, he suggests it can also be deliberately used to great effect for individuals, citing examples from clowns cheering up sick children in London hospitals to 'the feeling of new vitality which we experience after having seen an interesting theatrical performance' (p. 127).

Working at the same time, Russian psychiatrist Vladimir Iljine developed a form of therapeutic theatre. Although he knew of Evreinov and Stanislavski, Iljine worked mainly with mentally ill patients in hospitals. His major publications include *Improvising Theatre Play in the Treatment of Mood Disorders* (1909) and *Patients Play Theatre: A Way of Healing Body and Mind* (1910), in which he outlined his experience and theories.

After emigrating to Europe in the 1920s, Iljine encountered the work of psychoanalyst Sándor Ferenczi in Hungary. Ferenczi developed 'active techniques' in psychotherapy throughout the 1920s which influenced Iljine. These involved asking patients to perform certain enactments during analysis. In practising theatre therapy with individuals or groups, Iljine focused on improvisation, impromptu performance and the creation of scenarios around which improvisations might occur. Reflection or feedback phases allowed those involved to analyse their emotional experiences. Iljine connected mental illness to a loss of creativity, and therefore he aimed to reignite a creative spark in those he treated.

Psychodrama

These experiments in the use of theatre as a therapeutic tool find their most sustained development in the work of Romanian-born Jacob Levy Moreno, regarded by many as the founder of psychodrama. A psychiatrist who worked for most of his adult life in America, Moreno sought to extend Freud's ideas of individual analysis to include action methods and group therapy.

Moreno was familiar with Evreinov's *The Theatre in Life*, and Iljine translated Moreno's important text *The Theatre of Spontaneity* (1924) into Russian in 1925. Moving to the US in the same year, Moreno developed his practice with the general public at the Impromptu Theatre in Carnegie Hall, and in his involvement with prisons, psychiatric hospitals and residential treatment centres. In *The Theatre of Spontaneity*, Moreno outlines his ideas on the link he perceives between theatre and therapy. He focuses on three components: the spontaneous theatre, the living theatre and the therapeutic theatre, or theatre of catharsis. For Moreno and other psychodramatists, participation in carefully chosen dramatic scenarios and theatrical conventions can assist forms of mental illness and the working-through of emotional problems.

In 1932, Moreno introduced group psychotherapy to the American Psychiatric Association. In 1936, he created his first psychodrama theatre, at the Beacon Hill Sanatorium, New York. The American Society of Group Psychotherapy and Psychodrama (ASGPP) was founded in 1942. Over the course of forty years, Moreno researched paradigms for developing positive interpersonal relations within the fields of sociodrama, sociometry, sociatry and psychodrama.

Another important figure in this field is German-born Fritz Perls, who developed Gestalt therapy with his wife Laura Perls during the 1940s and 1950s, a process-oriented branch that prioritises feelings, sensations and perception. In the 1960s Perls became increasingly interested in the benefits of dramatic enactment within his practice. Influenced by Moreno's work on psychodrama, he began to include elements of it into his technique. Drawing on psychoanalytic, humanistic and cognitive approaches to therapy, Canadian Eric Berne developed Transactional Analysis in the 1950s. His book *Games People Play* (1964) expounds the different kinds of social performance we all engage in, and the ways in which interactive therapy might help address problematic patterns.

The British Psychodrama Association, established in 1984, advises that psychodrama can be engaged in for any number of reasons: personal, professional, therapeutic or training. In the West, Moreno is perhaps the most important figure in the early development and progression of psychodrama. His approaches are still used today in a variety of clinical settings. Although many see his praxis as distinct from dramatherapy, it shares clear links in its exploration of the therapeutic value of creative engagement.

Dramatherapy

Dramatherapy (UK) or Drama Therapy (US) has much in common with psychodrama insofar as the two disciplines use drama and theatre strategies as the basis for mental reflection and emotional healing. However, dramatherapists tend to be both artists and therapists, and the artistic process usually leads therapy.

In the first volume of *Drama as Therapy*, Phil Jones, a leading scholar in the field, defines dramatherapy in the following terms: 'The drama does not serve the therapy. The drama process contains the therapy' (p. 7). During dramatherapy sessions, participants 'make use of the *content* of drama activities, the *process* of creating enactments, and the *relationships* formed between those taking part in the work within a therapeutic framework' (p. 8). While psychodrama is one strategy within a broader therapeutic framework, dramatherapy draws on a range of drama and theatre devices. Core processes include projecting, empathising, distancing, role-playing, witnessing, movement and playing without consequence.

Many pioneering figures in dramatherapy are also involved with drama in education, a field with which I share the closest affinities, having worked as a specialist in schools for a number of years, including with theatre in education companies. The work of Peter Slade is seminal in this regard. Dedicated to 'Children everywhere, particularly the unhappy ones', Slade's important book *Child Drama* (1954) was the first major UK study to link drama with helping children develop emotionally and socially. Other studies duly built on the impact of Slade's work. For example, Brian Way's *Development through Drama* (1967) documents his work in educational drama from the 1940s until the 1960s.

Another important figure in the advancement of the therapeutic value of educational drama is Dorothy Heathcote, who began using drama as a teaching tool in UK schools, and also as a device to assist children with emotional and social problems in clinical settings.

In 1964 Marian Lindkvist founded the Sesame Institute to train drama movement therapists to work with people experiencing mental and emotional problems. The first training course in drama and movement therapy for occupational therapists was held at York Clinic, Guy's Hospital, London, in 1964. Influenced by the movement theories of Rudolf Laban, the psychoanalytic thought of Jung and Slade's work on drama in education, the institute focused on drama and movement as forms of learning and expression. Still in operation, it approaches mental health with a 'bias towards gesture, myth, and dream as being the first language of therapy and self-development' (Sesame Institute website).

The Sesame Institute provides an interesting case study to illustrate how dramatherapy sessions usually work. Typically, sessions follow a three-part structure. Participants have the opportunity to share their initial thoughts and feelings when they arrive, and this is followed by a warm-up. The core of the session involves dramatic exploration based on the needs of the individual or group, which might be established beforehand. Finally, there is a 'grounding' stage, in which people step out of roles, and have the opportunity to reflect upon the experience through verbal exchange.

Also bridging educational and clinical contexts, Sue Jennings began doing what she initially referred to as 'remedial drama' at a psychiatric hospital in Warwick, UK, in the 1950s, when she was a drama student. In the 1970s, after completing a PhD in anthropology, Jennings started to call her work 'dramatherapy', and she has since become a leading figure in the development of drama in education and dramatherapy worldwide. Indeed, Jennings has also been central in the development of play therapy. This distinct discipline, which I do not treat in depth here because of obvious restrictions, is a person-centred approach to therapy rooted in the work of Anna Freud and Melanie Klein, and also drawing heavily on the work of Carl Rogers and Virginia M. Axline. Jennings' most recent work, *Healthy Attachments and Neuro-Dramatic-Play* (2011), yokes together drama and neurology in developing the concept of 'neuro-dramatic-play', which she sees as emerging in the second half of pregnancy and the first few months after birth. She claims this mother–child interaction, which is essentially 'dramatic' in nature, is crucial for brain development and healthy interpersonal attachments.

Theatric therapies

Given that psychodrama and dramatherapy aim to effect some kind of change in individuals or groups, or at least to cultivate positive affective experiences, they have something in common with other socially and politically engaged theatre movements of the twentieth century. The figure perhaps most representative of the marriage of the psychological and the socio-political in theatre practice is the Brazilian theatre artist, writer and politician Augusto Boal. Drawing on his experience of Stanislavski training at the Actors Studio in New York, as well as the libertarian philosophy of Paulo Freire, Boal developed a model of interactive theatre that bridged the psychic and the social called 'Theatre of the Oppressed', which was largely developed with the poor of São Paulo in the 1950s and 1960s. Boal created experiences that mobilised dialogue, interaction and physical movement, and were designed to give those with whom he worked more control over their life choices and circumstances. He used the word 'spect-actor' to describe those who both watched and took action in this theatre.

Writing in *The Aesthetics of the Oppressed* (2006), with reference to Aristotle's writing on tragedy, Boal notes that empathy emerges when the protagonist learns the truth of his situation, such as when Oedipus realises that he has killed his father and married his mother. This moment of recognition is a key rational and ethical point in tragic theatre, but Boal claims that empathy should also be tied to action. Catharsis risks reproducing the status quo unless it is harnessed to propel change, in Boal's approach. Hollywood movies exemplify this danger, he charges, insofar as they produce 'pure empathy to brutalise their spectators' (p. 54, n. 17). For the psychic and social to connect, the individual must do something with her feelings; she must translate emotion into action.

In *The Rainbow of Desire* (1995), Boal states that Theatre of the Oppressed is interested in educational, social and therapeutic goals (p. 15). He elaborates on the therapeutic dimension, mainly outlining his use of image theatre to explore subjective experiences. As Adrian Jackson observes in the introduction to the book, this represents Boal's move from democratising theatre to democratising therapy, where catharsis takes the form of disassembling societal constructions and dynamising repressed desire (pp. xxi–xxii). For Boal, what he refers to as 'theatric therapies' involve people taking charge of a course of action in view of others:

> The importance of theatric therapies ... resides essentially in the mechanism of transformation of the protagonist, who moves from being object-subject of social but also psychological forces, conscious and unconscious forces, to become the subject of this object-subject – which is the work of the patient. (p. 27)

Targeting educational, social and therapeutic issues, Boal is not interested in neat disciplinary distinctions. For him, theatre can be therapeutic without being formalised therapy. As he states in a 2004 interview with Stig A. Eriksson and Mette Bøe Lyngstad, 'My comment is that theatre is therapeutic, it is not therapy but it is therapeutic ... Therapy assumes that you have a psychological problem and a need for treatment. Therapy also assumes that there is a therapist, a person who knows better than us' (pp. 1–2).

While some people believe that Boal's work is utopian, it has perhaps been the most influential approach to developing socially engaged theatre projects worldwide. His theatre considers context, environment, physical participation and critical reflection to be crucial to personal and socio-political transformation. In this sense, his conception of what counts as therapeutic is quite nuanced and complex, for the individual is always perceived and engaged in relation to a socio-political context. In the next section we will continue to look at some of the varied and challenging ways in which the idea of the therapeutic inflects contemporary theatre and performance practice. We will pay particular attention to modes of reimagining and framing catharsis, which while not identical to Boalian ideals, nonetheless invite us to think about other ways in which theatre and performance effects and affects us.

Therapeutic dramaturgies and relations in contemporary theatre

So far we have looked at some of the more obvious and direct associations between theatre and therapy. Side-stepping this trajectory somewhat, this section examines a range of contemporary theatre and performance practices that expand the idea of 'the therapeutic' by centralising confession, physical and emotional intimacy, and affective experience as dramaturgical principles. It also explores ways in which theatre processes and practices can be seen to create spaces for writers and theatre-makers, solo performers, audiences and communities to negotiate mental and emotional experience. Often, these divisions collapse into one another, but they are nonetheless useful for exploring the various ways in which the therapeutic emerges as a creative strategy and a relational mode of address and engagement.

At the outset of this book I promised to discuss what I discern as contemporary ways of imagining catharsis in theatre and performance. To return to this issue now, one way we might perceive the therapeutic mode which I'm highlighting is as an evolved form of Aristotelian catharsis that reflects the varied, complex ways we now understand theatre and performance to effect and affect us. While Aristotle's model of catharsis largely presumes the spectator's concentrated identification with certain characters or narrative, as indeed does Freud's writing on tragedy, developments in theatre and performance during the twentieth and twenty-first centuries (in the work of Artaud, Brecht and Boal, for instance) suggest that engagement is more complicated than a process of identification and emotional purgation. This shift in understanding is also reflected to varying degrees by research in psychology and neurology, as well as studies of affect, which suggest that we process experience not according to mind/body, intellectual/emotional divisions, but in more layered, integrated ways. (See Antonio R. Damasio, *Descartes' Error: Emotion, Reason, and the Human Brain*, 1994; Bruce McConachie, *Engaging Audiences: A Cognitive Approach to Spectating in the Theatre*, 2008; and Erin Hurley, *Theatre & Feeling*, 2010.)

In *Relational Aesthetics* (1998) Nicolas Bourriaud understands relational art to refer to processes and practices, mainly taking shape in the 1990s, which focus on human relations and their social contexts. Similarly, with regard to theatre and performance, we might take the term 'relational' to refer to work that is primarily invested in exploring intra- and interpersonal relationships in certain social spheres, such as the examples profiled in this section. What I see as a heightened interest in this dynamic may have something to do with our immersion in the kind of narcissistic therapy culture I discussed in the first section. However, it may also have something to do with a legitimate need to check in on our emotional states, and the relationships that effect and affect them, in a highly globalised, digitised world where the lines between private and public, real and imaginary, here and there, self and other seem increasingly blurred and complicated. It is against this backdrop that the theatre and performance considered in this section seems to me especially resonant and relevant. Less preoccupied with a formal attachment to therapy, it experiments with dramaturgical and relational structures to explore its own healing, soothing or simply affirming potential.

Writers and theatre-makers

As a dramatic form, the monologue is as much a confession as it is a story. In the 1990s, particularly in Ireland and the UK, it enjoyed something of a renaissance. One of the playwrights to repeatedly exploit this form is Conor McPherson. When the device appears in his drama, typically it is used by troubled male characters to reveal their most private thoughts to the audience. Its function, therefore, seems to be as something of a talking cure for the distressed character, who is given a rare opportunity to speak directly to an attentive group of people.

In McPherson's earliest play, *Rum and Vodka* (1992), a twenty-four-year-old man speaks alone on stage about his unhappy marriage and lost youth. He got his current wife pregnant one night while he was drunk, married her, and when the play opens has two children, a house and an office job he hates. To block out emotional pain he has started to drink heavily. His story is a web of disappointment and frustration which both alcohol and the theatre format allow him to share. Confessions such as his are not easy to make within the macho, working-class milieu in which he was born and lives, and so the monologue format provides a platform for the revelation of highly sensitive, private information.

This Lime Tree Bower (1995) relies upon a similar dramaturgy, although here three young men from south Dublin sit on chairs to confess their disaffection to the audience, and maybe to each other – although this possibility is only implied by their proximity on stage. Again, the monologue format seems to allow men in particular the opportunity to articulate thoughts and feelings that they otherwise struggle to share, either because no one listens or because their stoic masculinity is at risk of being compromised.

The theatre critic who speaks directly to the audience in McPherson's *St. Nicholas* (1997) does not let the complexity of the monologue form go unaddressed. 'There's always going to be a smugness about you listening to this,' he says. 'These restrictions, these rules, they give us that freedom. I have the freedom to tell you this unhindered, while you can sit there assured that no one is going to get hurt. Possibly offended, but you'll live. We're all quite safe here' (p. 160). Interestingly, here the main character seems to wilfully manipulate the confessional mode, while the audience knows that nothing dangerous is going to happen on stage. We may be inadvertently cast as his therapists, and it is ostensibly our role to listen, but we are assured that nothing will seriously affect us.

McPherson's *Shining City*, which opened at the Royal Court, London, in 2004, also explores the link between theatre and therapy. Although characters speak to each other in the play, most of the dialogue includes inexperienced therapist Ian, a former priest who has just set up the new clinic in which we find him. In this layered history of roles, McPherson illuminates a connection between the function of religious confession, therapeutic dialogue and the theatre event itself. Characters enter to try to vocalise their anguish to the priest/therapist, while the audience keeps an eye on all involved.

At the heart of this drama is widower John, who has been experiencing visions of his wife Mari, who recently died in a car crash. In these scenarios she tries to speak. Such is John's difficulty with communication that he himself struggles to fully articulate this dimension to the visions. In the tradition of *Hamlet*, the ghost he claims to see but who cannot speak is more of a metaphor for his own difficulties in processing grief. Not until he can talk about it will he find peace. The curative potential of talk also inflects Ian's conversations with the play's other two characters – his girlfriend Neasa and the young father Laurence. Although the therapist might be the legitimate figure who listens in this play, McPherson also seems to suggest that both religious and theatrical practices can serve similar purposes.

The relationship between grief and confession recurs as a dramaturgical strategy and as a mode of address in David Hare's adaptation of Joan Didion's *The Year of Magical Thinking* (2005). Didion's memoir was compiled during the year following the death of her husband, and adapted by the author for the stage under Hare's direction. While the novel pursues an intimate, diary-like format, the production resembles a public confession.

In the first stage production of the play, at the Booth Theatre New York in 2007, Vanessa Redgrave channelled Didion's story. Writing about the experience in *The New York Times*, Didion recalls being asked whether she found it strange being played by Redgrave. She reports replying: 'Vanessa Redgrave is not playing me, Vanessa Redgrave is playing a character who, for the sake of clarity, is called Joan Didion' (4 March 2007). In this instance, it appears that for the writer whose deeply personal experience is being relayed, it was strategically necessary to filter grief through a performer playing a character, rather than a version of herself.

Dublin-based writer and performer Neil Watkins queered Didion's memoir with his solo performance *The Year of Magical Wanking*, which opened at Project Arts Centre in 2010, directed by Phillip McMahon, and has since toured internationally with THISISPOPBABY production company. Watkins' is a story of self-harm, sex addition and HIV infection delivered on a stark set, in rhyme. Unlike Didion's work, Watkins' is a fast-paced, graphic and hard-hitting performance that invokes religious narrative and symbology to frame his tale of redemption through a mixture of healing rituals and theatre-making over the course of a year. As the opening address of his performance reveals, Watkins' addiction spurs him to make art, in which his self-expressed problems can be further addressed and examined:

> I am Neil Martin Watkins and I am
> A sex and love addicted innocent.
> There's patterns I've adopted that would taint
>   the Love of Saints.
> I wank, therefore I slam.

While Watkins' story is certainly personal, the confessional mode he adopts has become quite pervasive in contemporary Irish theatre, where it has been frequently deployed by theatre-makers in the past five years to expose incidents of physical and sexual abuse by members of the Catholic Church throughout the twentieth century. (See also, for example, the work of Brokentalkers.)

While the dramatic monologue privileges a character's direct disclosure of private experience, it also offers the audience a unique opportunity to listen. According to Adam Phillips, writing about psychoanalysis in *Equals* (2002), the value of listening in therapy is often downgraded next to talking: 'Calling psychoanalysis a talking cure has obscured the sense in which it is a listening cure (and the senses in which it is not a cure at all). Being listened to can enable oneself to bear — and even to enjoy — listening to oneself and others' (p. xii). Following on, we can say that while theatre talk such as the monologue forms discussed above allows characters to express their private thoughts, in a reflexive sense, for the audience member, careful listening might also prove beneficial.

Solo performers

With the dramatic monologue, writers create characters to be embodied by performers. In the case of *The Year of Magical Thinking*, a writer's grief is filtered through an actor's performance. However, many live or performance artists deliberately use their own stories and bodies as the basis for intimate exchange.

In 2005, the Dublin-based theatre company Pan Pan produced the large-scale project *One: Healing with Theatre*. The primary aim of this production was to devote attention to the motivations and experiences of actors. Over the course of a year, the company's artistic director Gavin Quinn visited the homes of 100 performers, asking each of them: 'Why do you think you became an actor?'

Each actor's response was filmed and photographed and later used in a live performance encounter. The film, which shadowed the performers in their homes, had an outdoor public airing at Meeting House Square in the city centre. Still photographs were included in a large book of the same title. The filmic and photographic component of the project attempted to render visible and dignify the often-undervalued lives of jobbing actors. This was their therapy.

While actors were central to the development of this piece, the relationship between performer and spectator was at the heart of the live performance event. In a large space with 100 separate rooms, one member of the public joined each performer. The actors explained to the listener-witnesses why they became professional performers. While this format still privileged the actor's experience, participants could interact if they wanted to, so that the live exchange was much more reciprocal. Even though the project titularly aimed to 'heal', Pan Pan essentially played with formal therapeutic conventions to explore the possibility and value of sharing experience in aesthetically organised performance contexts.

While Pan Pan's project comprised numerous individual performers, UK-based Bobby Baker works almost exclusively as a solo performer and visual artist. Much of Baker's performance and visual art deals with personal experiences of mental illness. For Baker, art is a way of exploring and explaining mental illness and its treatment.

Many of Baker's early performance pieces investigate the connection between femininity, motherhood, food and domestic life. However, more recent work has directly broached the subject of mental health. In *How to Live* (2004), which was funded by the Wellcome Trust and first performed in full at the Barbican, London, Baker pursues a lecture-style format to investigate mental health and its treatment. She wittily instructs the audience how to tell the difference between psychiatrists, psychoanalysts and psychologists on the basis of the shoes they wear.

Baker then proceeds to enact a therapeutic scenario with her unlikely patient, a giant pea that has been diagnosed with a personality disorder. The pea is unwilling to speak in front of the audience, and Baker manipulates the scenario in a scaled model of the therapy setting, which is filmed and mediated on a large screen for the audience to see. Dressed as a giant pea herself, and using film, stills and story, Baker teaches the pea/patient skills necessary for positive mental health:

1. Breath
2. Exercise
3. Assertiveness
4. Exposure
5. Mindfulness
6. Adult Pleasant Event Schedule
7. Acting Opposite to the Emotion
8. Chain Analysis
9. Validation
10. Interpersonal Effectiveness
11. Charm

Reflecting on this performance in *Bobby Baker: Redeeming Features of Daily Life* (2007), the artist remarks that she initially wanted to 'poke fun' at the treatment she had been undertaking in America, 'the world of therapies, their inventors and websites' (p. 77). Her comments reveal something about the extent to which therapy has now become big business. Although there may be many useful medical and psychological approaches for responding to mental health issues, we get a sense in Baker's work that therapy culture, as an industry, can be exploitative and actually perpetuate poor mental health, and that our medical institutions can fail us. Baker wants to offer an antidote to this: 'I wanted to create my own "therapy" as a subversive commentary' (p. 77). Yet Baker's approach does not aim to neatly classify mental suffering; nor does it expect us to do so. As Deirdre Heddon remarks in the essay 'Box Story' (2007), the performer's 'stories are neither intended to provide a truth about the world, nor about the person who tells the story. They are merely one pragmatic response to the actual lived, messy experiences of life' (p. 237).

Baker's diary drawings represent her most sustained artistic response to mental illness. She started compiling them in 1996 when she first visited a psychiatrist, and continued to illustrate her experiences while attending a local authority day centre in London. Many have been publicly displayed since, including in a major exhibition at the Wellcome Trust which opened in March 2009 titled *Bobby Baker's Diary Drawings: Mental Illness and Me, 1997–2008*. For Baker, art assisted her in recovery. As she tells Anna Bawden in interview, 'Recovery is about communicating, so if my pictures can communicate with people in some way, that's great' (*The Guardian*, 18 March 2009).

Humour is one the key strategies Baker deploys in her performances to broach issues around mental health. Freud recognised the role comedy plays in processing painful or traumatic repressed experiences. In *Jokes and Their*

Relation to the Unconscious (1905), he suggests that what is funny is often what has been socially repressed and that jokes succeed in 'lifting inhibition' (p. 158). When adults engage in comic play, Freud claims, their egos weaken, allowing buried impulses to emerge. The link between comedy and therapy is perhaps most apparent in stand-up performance.

It is something of a cliché to say that most comedians are also manic depressives, yet it is hard to ignore that quite a number of stand-ups make this claim themselves. Ruby Wax is a comedian who has been especially outspoken about her depression, recently developing the show *Ruby Wax: Losing It* around the subject. Both instructive and funny, Wax's show includes factual information about mental illness (including opportunities to meet with mental health professionals in the theatre during the show's run) and anecdotes drawn from her own experience. Wax claims she 'lost it' in 2004 and was admitted to the Priory clinic in London, where she undertook group therapy. In 2006, she went back to college to gain a postgraduate diploma in psychotherapy and counselling, and in 2010 began a master's degree in mindfulness-based cognitive therapy at Oxford University.

In *Ruby Wax: Losing It*, the comedian draws on all these personal and professional experiences to create a witty and educational form of group therapy. The premise is that people with mental illness often pass through life without a manual, and Wax's show aims to act as a steering intervention. The piece was first performed at the Priory before a

UK tour in 2011, during which I saw the show at the Menier Chocolate Factory, London.

Wax is accompanied on stage by singer-songwriter friend Judith Owen on piano, who has also experienced depression, and the first part of the show is a cabaret-style comedy in which Wax confesses her mental health problems, while humorously enacting her breakdown. In the second half there's room for questions and answers with the audience. 'One in four of us suffer from mental illness,' Wax repeats throughout. In this production we see how comic performance becomes the means by which a personal account of mental illness and its treatment is relayed in a safe, non-threatening way, and the light-hearted live event creates the conditions for the easy exchange of experience and information. As Wax wryly remarks in interview with Jasper Rees, 'If depressives laugh, you know you've got a hit' (*The Telegraph*, 6 April 2010).

Some organisations have sought to harness the connection between comedy and mental health in a more on-going, systematic way. Stand Up For Mental Health (SMH) was founded in Vancouver, Canada, in 2004 with the intention of assisting people with mental illness by teaching them stand-up as a form of supplemental therapy. Under the guidance of author and comedian David Granirer, who lives with depression, participants develop routines in order to feel better about themselves and raise awareness among their audiences. These routines are performed at conferences and treatment centres, in the offices of various mental health organisations and government agencies, and for the general public around Canada.

Granirer claims that comedy helps 'reduce the stigma and discrimination around mental illness'. He maintains that 'laughing at our setbacks raises us above them. It makes people go from despair to hope, and hope is crucial to any-one struggling with adversity'. While he is mindful of the fact that stand-up alone cannot resolve serious mental health problems, Granirer states that it has curative benefits: 'There's something incredibly healing about telling a room-ful of people exactly who you are and having them laugh and cheer' (SMH website, 4 May 2011). The organisation has also targeted specific community groups, and in 2010 developed a programme for sex workers with mental illness in conjunction with Prostitution Alternatives Counselling & Education (PACE) Society in Vancouver. In recognition of the group's achievements, it received a $50,000 sponsor-ship from Canada Post in 2010.

More recently still, the worlds of comedy and therapy have been formally brought together at the famous Laugh Factory in Los Angeles. In February 2011, owner Jamie Masada hired clinical psychologist Dr Ildiko Tabori to work on-site with the comedians who perform at his venue. The stand-ups receive the free sessions on Groucho Marx's former couch.

Masada, who has worked at the club for more than thirty years, saw this intervention as necessary because many of the club's performers suffered from serious mental health issues. Speaking in interview, he highlights the extent of the problem, noting: 'From Richard Jeni putting a gun in his mouth and blowing himself up to Greg Giraldo taking drugs and overdosing ... From Sam Kinison to Rodney Dangerfield to Paul Rodriguez, Dom Irrera – every comic, they have a little demon in them' (cited by Deborah Vankin in the *Los Angeles Times*, 9 February 2011).

In the first volume of *The History of Sexuality: The Will to Knowledge* (1976), French philosopher Michel Foucault criticises psychiatry and psychoanalysis for claiming to reveal the truth about human subjects. For Foucault, this pressure to confess is distinctly Christian in nature, and merely enables the production of a subject who might be known and thus controlled. In the third volume, *The Care of the Self* (1984), Foucault proposes that we need to develop new relational modes. While an element of confession is central to the strategies deployed in the performances described in the previous paragraphs, unlike with religion and therapy, there is no master discourse available to make sense of the theatrical experience. If, following Foucault, we were to describe the ethics of these post-Christian or post-Freudian performances, we might be struck by the manner in which they simply centralise thoughtful, careful encounters with others.

Audiences

As I have outlined above, writers and performers can use theatre and performance to process and share their experiences in a manner that resembles the therapeutic encounter. While audiences may engage with work in numerous unpredictable ways, in the examples mentioned in this section so far we see how the spectator not only watches theatre, but is often deliberately cast in the role of therapist/listener. In thinking further about the therapeutic shades of contemporary theatre and performance, I would like to continue by exploring the role of physical and emotional intimacy in the structuring of live encounters.

Adrian Howells' practice is representative of the way in which performance can pursue an intensely intimate trajectory, drawing on both religious and therapeutic ideas of confession and associated absolution or healing. Howells typically works with individuals or small groups of people in everyday environments – living rooms, launderettes, hairdressers, for example – and his practice considers the possibility of intimacy in performance. As stated in an article co-authored with Deirdre Heddon, 'From Talking to Silence: A Confessional Journey' (2011), Howells is motivated by 'the therapeutic benefits of confession', citing as his mantra 'a burden shared is a burden halved' (p. 2).

In *Adrienne's Living Room*, created for an Arena 10 show in London in 2002, Howells adopts the female persona Adrienne. Initially set in a warehouse, the performance space was transformed into Adrienne's living room, full of kitsch mementos and camp objects, night-lights and incense. A small group gathers, and during the course of the evening they drink tea, eat biscuits, play games and chat with Howells. Although it was an early experiment in working with this kind of theatre, Howells recalls how he basically 'wanted people to feel in some way "lighter" by the time they left me, that it might be about a "problem shared is a problem halved" and that would be a significant experience of tea and sympathy' ('Being Adrienne ... ', 2005). The performance turned into a form of confessional theatre as people relaxed and grew keen to share their secrets.

This style of frank exchange also characterises *Adrienne's Dirty Laundry Experience*, created for the Arches Theatre, Glasgow, in 2003. The performance is set in a working launderette, and the small group assembled are encouraged to share metaphorical 'dirty laundry' as their clothes are washed. In the one-on-one performance *Salon Adrienne* (2005), set in a hairdressing salon, Howells washes each participant's hair while also prompting reflection about self-perception. He gives Indian head massages, and in his own words 'teases' participants' hair while asking personal questions. Here R. D. Laing's conviction that therapists must help unravel the 'knotty' problems that patients bring to the clinic is given application in a rather concrete though playful way.

In *Adrienne: The Great Depression* (2004), first performed at the Great Eastern Hotel, London, Howells reflects upon his personal experience of severe depression.

For this piece the performer spends one week in a hotel room, which he does not leave. With the curtains closed, Howells allows day to fold into night, as cutlery from room service mounts up. Performing as Adrienne, he does not remove his make-up; nor does he shave or wash. Throughout the week, Howells posts photographs and a stream-of-consciousness text on the walls, until the space seems to embody his psychic state. Audience-participants are admitted to the room, and Howells speaks candidly of his suicidal feelings.

Taking a more physical approach, in the one-on-one site-specific performance *Held* (2006) Howells actively holds individual participants at different degrees of closeness, and in different rooms, moving from hand-holding to spoon-ing. In this piece, structured around a haptic dramaturgy, the performer explores the connection between perform-ance, intimacy and space. Reflecting on the experience on his research webpage at the University of Glasgow, Howells claims that 'the structures of confession may be about bod-ily conversations or exchanges as much as the oral/aural: the place of exchange may matter less than the form of exchange'. In this observation, Howells impresses on us the idea that theatre and performance encounters can act as powerful physical and emotional 'holding' spaces, to use Winnicott's description of supportive environments. Of course, these encounters do not feel supportive to every-one. Many people will feel that this kind of interaction in performance is too intense, and even exploitative. In my experience of Howells at least, the nature of the experience is clearly signalled beforehand so that would-be participants can make informed decisions about whether or not they want to take part.

Foot Washing for the Sole (2008) combines verbal and physical interaction in a one-on-one performance. Inspired by the Judaeo-Christian practice of washing feet, Howells washes and dries each participant's feet, before anointing and massaging them with oil. As I entered the space in Kilkenny in 2010, Howells asked some questions about my well-being and my relationship to my feet, and suggested how one might correspond service with love. Finally, he asked for permission to kiss my feet. Here, the piece unites Judaeo-Christian and Freudian traditions in a performance of talking and touching.

Many of Howells' signature strategies are channelled into one of his most recent works, *The Pleasure of Being: Washing, Feeding, Holding*, which was first performed at the Battersea Arts Festival in 2010. In this piece, the artist bathes participants in a rose-filled bath, dries them, offers chocolate and cradles them for a time. This encounter is remarkably different from the confessional, psychologically textured work which I have been tracing so far. Instead, here we can see Howells extend our understanding of the therapeutic by hinting that wordless, physical experiences can also be deeply affecting. This is reflected in the arc of his work to date, which reveals a shift from verbal exchange to intimate bodily co-presence.

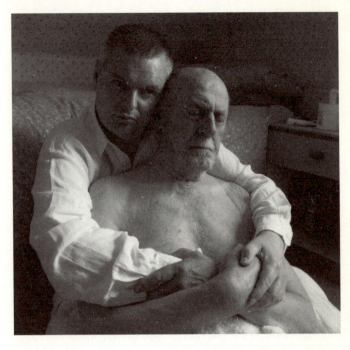

Touch therapy: Adrian Howells holds participant, *The Pleasure of Being: Washing, Feeding, Holding* (2010). Photo by Hamish Barton. (Used with kind permission of Howells.)

The performer David Hoyle has also played with the therapy format in his work. In 2009, Hoyle led *Dave's Drop-in Centre* at the Vauxhall Tavern, London, a pub (and at one time during the nineteenth-century a molly house) which hosts a range of queer and cabaret performances. While Hoyle often speaks directly to audience members in his work, this series of six shows was specifically constructed around an interactive therapeutic scenario. In interview with Nancy Durrant, Hoyle explains that it was 'loosely inspired by a psychiatric daycare centre … and all the activities that go on, from occupational therapy to hobbies to empowerment, group catharsis' (*The Sunday Times*, 21 April 2009).

As a gay performer who typically plays to queer audiences in bars and theatres, Hoyle often deals with sexual matters in his work. Open about being seriously bullied as child because of his sexuality, he regularly tackles issues of poor self-image and self-esteem among his audience. Frequently interacting with spectators, Hoyle is interested in closing the distance between the performer and the spectator in social spaces, exploiting the scenario as a basis for dialogue. Hoyle performed as Divine David until 2000. In an ice-show spectacular at Streatham's Ice Arena, he killed off his alter ego and took a six-year break from performing during which he undertook therapy. That experience feeds into the Vauxhall performance.

At the opening of Hoyle's first 'Drop-in Centre' show on 30 April 2009, the performer announces, 'This is a psychiatric day centre … It's not about any one of you cunts. It's about us as a collective.' Including a range of guest performers, and drawing on interactive discussion, singing and painting, the performances challenge the self-loathing, narcissism and complacency that Hoyle perceives among the gay community. Marrying cabaret with Theatre of Cruelty aesthetics, Hoyle's method is raucous and sometimes quite shocking as he shouts at the audience, throws paint or draws with his own blood. Hoyle wants his spectators to share with him and engage with one another, although he is more likely to insist than to coax. This does not stop his work from being intensely affecting, whether in exposing some kind of social taboo or engaging spectators in really honest exchanges. The psychiatric daycare centre may be his starting point, but Hoyle transforms the social space of a London pub into a place where defences are dropped, if not bludgeoned, and you come away feeling all the better for it.

Even though many people will see Hoyle's performances as risqué, and even insensitive towards spectators, he seems to genuinely aim to positively affect people's lives. A group of performers who are less transparent in their intentions are the Belgian collective Ontroerend Goed. To date, this company has chiefly probed the boundaries of intimacy in performance, often by drawing analogies between therapy, dating and interrogation.

In *Internal*, first performed in 2009, five performers each select one participant of their choosing, and lead them to separate booths. When I attended the show in Dublin in 2010, Maria took me with her. She offered me vodka, flirted outrageously, shared ostensibly personal stories and attempted to seduce me into doing the same. After about ten minutes, I was brought into the centre of the room, where I and the other nine performers and participants gathered in a circle. Here, whatever trust had been built or naively assumed was shattered when the performers shared our secrets and undermined our responses in a kind of brutal group therapy encounter. 'Fintan values friendship a great deal,' Maria told the group, 'but he is stiff like a Ken doll.' As in *A Game of You*, which also played at this time, in which isolated participants' secrets and observations are unwittingly recorded and replayed for the consumption of others, Ontroerend Goed seem to be warning us against the pervasive cultural imperative to share our feelings so readily. I, for one, learned the hard way.

Communities

Many people who take part in participatory and collaborative theatre and performance practices attest to the benefits for their well-being. Some socially engaged theatre initiatives, for example, while specifically striving to empower disadvantaged groups, centralise the sharing of personal experience in the creation and presentation of performance. Although many of these projects are driven by social justice rather than therapeutic goals, frequently there is plenty of cross-over between processes, practices and objectives.

Theatre of Witness projects are especially representative of the overlap between socially and psychologically engaged theatre and performance. Originally intended as creative peace initiatives, they aimed to help those affected by conflict and violence. Whereas Theatre of Testimony builds professional productions around historical events, Theatre of Witness programmes centralise the experiences of individuals shared in the devising process, leading to intimate public performances following which issues of shared concern can be discussed among those present.

Developed by dancer and counsellor Teya Sepinuck, Theatre of Witness productions have been taking place since 1986, focusing at different stages on the experiences of refugees, immigrants, survivors and perpetrators of domestic abuse, prisoners and the families of murder victims. In 2009, The Playhouse in Derry began a Theatre of Witness project to explore the impact of the so-called Troubles on communities and generations of people in the North. The project has resulted in two productions: *We Carried Your Secrets* (2009) and *I Once Knew a Girl* (2010).

Those who participated in the development workshops in Derry spoke of the profound healing they experienced in the course of their involvement, and this sentiment was frequently shared by the audience. Often, relatives of people on stage who came to see the presentation spoke of not having known how their loved ones felt up until that point, and on other occasions conversations developed around the events documented. What started with the experiences of individuals turned into a sharing of experience for audiences and, in regional touring, entire communities. Describing how one audience member questioned the ethics of the format at a performance of *We Carried Your Secrets* on 4 December 2010, during which one spectator became extremely distressed, David Grant writes, 'Although this in no way lessened the mutual discomfort of his exposure, it confronted us with the plain truth that understanding requires disclosure' (*Irish Theatre Magazine*, 4 December 2010). What seems crucial is that the artistic solicitation and presentation of the material is done in such a way that those most affected might take ownership of its negotiation after the show. Appreciated in this light, the idea of the therapeutic is not mired in the subjective. Instead, the theatrical framing of individual experience can assist in the cultural processing of trauma.

Conclusion

In the West, Freudian psychoanalysis may have provided one of the first sustained paradigms to champion the value of clinically structured talking and listening to mental and emotional well-being, but other branches of psychology, and readers of Freud's work, have since re-evaluated or nuanced this approach to therapy. A case in point, Adam Phillips is keen to counter Freud's insistence that psychoanalysis is a science. In his book *On Flirtation* (1996), Phillips compares it to a form of 'practical poetry' (p. xi), or as the literary critic Tim Dean says, 'an experiment in conversation' (*Traffic East Magazine*, 2007).

Moreover, acknowledging how expensive therapy is, and even how hard to access, Phillips champions its democratisation, while conceding that there are many things people might do to improve well-being other than entering therapy. In an interview with Alain de Botton in *The Telegraph*, he says: 'for me, psychoanalysis is only one among many things you might do if you're feeling unwell – you might also try aromatherapy, knitting, hang-gliding. There are lots of things you can do with your distress. I don't believe psychoanalysis is the best thing you can do, even if I value it a great deal' (7 April 2011).

In this book I have argued that theatre and therapy share many historical, conceptual and practical connections by focusing on some points of contact and divergence between the aims, practices, effects and affects of the disciplines. In the first section we saw how many of the leading figures who developed therapeutic theories and techniques in the late nineteenth and early twentieth centuries looked to tragic Greek and Shakespearian theatre to develop their ideas. We also discovered how psychology influenced Naturalist and Surrealist theatre, and, in the theatre of Artaud, informed anti-psychological, somatic approaches to performance. Subsequent sections traced the ways in which ideas from therapy informed approaches to actor training and audience engagement, and the manner in which drama and theatre has been directly harnessed within therapeutic contexts. In this final section we looked at contemporary theatre and performance practice that is less interested in the tragic or well-made play as a source of psychological insight and impact. Instead of staging narrative action to be watched from a distance, the work examined centralises confession, intimacy and an affective vitality within the live encounter, and in this respect can be understood to advance neo-Aristotelian ideas of catharsis.

Finally, to play with Phillips' description of therapy as practical poetry, we might say that in the contemporary work analysed in this last section we see examples of the embodied, practical therapeutic investigations and innovations of theatre. However experimental or aspirational these processes and practices might be, a therapeutic dramaturgy informs the organisation of the performances in question, while a therapeutic relation structures the live performance encounters. Theatre dialogues with therapy, positing itself as a related, if not an alternative practice for gaining insight into ourselves and our relationships. In a great deal of the work discussed here, the whole idea of what counts as therapy is both implicitly and explicitly interrogated, and embodied encounters with theatre and performance, rather than medical or clinical intervention, are the stimuli for mental and emotional awareness, reflection and well-being.

further reading

Theatre & Therapy explores some intersections between theatre and therapy by looking at four key strands or points of contact between the disciplines: their shared traditions, perspectives on actor training and audience engagement, theatre as a tool within psychodrama and dramatherapy, and ways of understanding the dramaturgical choices and therapeutic relations particular to a range of contemporary theatre and performance practices. Suffice to say, each section is worthy of its own bibliography.

Despite the breadth and complexity of these intersections, readers may find certain titles particularly useful for further study. Those interested in learning more about theatre and the therapeutic tradition, and ways of exploring theatre and performance through a psychoanalytic prism, will find Patrick Campbell and Adrian Kear's edited collection *Psychoanalysis and Performance* (2001) invaluable.

Joseph Roach's *The Player's Passion: Studies in the Science of Acting* (1993) offers superb insight into how approaches to acting have been influenced throughout history by scientific theories of the body. Broaching similar territory, while focusing on Stanislavski's legacy, Jonathan Pitches' *Science and the Stanislavsky Tradition of Acting* (2006) is also an important resource.

Phil Jones offers a wonderful overview of key histories and debates in psychotherapy and dramatherapy in the two volumes of *Drama as Therapy: Theory, Practice and Research* (2007) and *Clinical Work and Research into Practice* (2010).

A more cautious note sounds from Frank Furedi's *Therapy Culture: Cultivating Vulnerability in an Uncertain Age* (2004), in which the author warns of the dangers of framing experience in therapeutic terms.

As stated at the outset, this book primarily focuses on Western theatre and therapeutic traditions (particularly Freudian, and its legacy), and readers interested in other cultural contexts or disciplinary paradigms will have to search beyond the remit of this study.

Aristotle. *Poetics*. Trans. Malcolm Heath. London: Penguin, 1996.

Artaud, Antonin. *The Theatre and Its Double*. 1938. Trans. Mary Caroline Richards. New York: Grove, 1958.

Baker, Bobby, and Michèle Barrett, eds. *Bobby Baker: Redeeming Features of Daily Life*. London: Routledge, 2007.

Bawden, Anna. 'The Art of Surviving Mental Illness' [interview with Bobby Baker]. *The Guardian* 18 March 2009. <http://www.guardian.co.uk/society/2009/mar/18/mental-health-bobby-baker-exhibition>.

Blau, Herbert. *The Audience*. Baltimore, MD: Johns Hopkins UP, 1990.

Boal, Augusto. *The Aesthetics of the Oppressed*. Trans. Adrian Jackson. London: Routledge, 2006.

————. *The Rainbow of Desire: The Boal Method of Theatre and Therapy*. Trans. Adrian Jackson. London: Routledge, 1995.

Bollas, Christopher. *Hysteria*. London: Routledge, 2000.

Bourriaud, Nicolas. *Relational Aesthetics*. 1998. Trans. Simon Pleasance and Fronza Woods. Dijon: Les Presses du Réel, 2002.

Breton, André. 'Surrealist Manifesto.' 1924. <http://www.tcf.ua.edu/Classes/Jbutler/T340/SurManifesto/ManifestoOfSurrealism.htm>.

Campbell, Patrick, and Adrian Kear, eds. *Psychoanalysis and Performance*. London: Routledge, 2001.

Carlson, Marvin. *The Haunted Stage: Theatre as Memory Machine*. Ann Arbor: U of Michigan P, 2003.

Cixous, Hélène. 'The Name of Oedipus: Song of the Forbidden Body'. 1978. *Plays by French and Francophone Women: A Critical Anthology*. Ed. Christiane Makward and Judith G. Miller. Ann Arbor: U of Michigan P, 1995. 247–326.

————. 'Portrait of Dora'. 1976. Trans. Ann Liddle. *The Selected Plays of Hélène Cixous*. Ed. Eric Prenowitz. London: Routledge, 2004. 35–60.

Damasio, Antonio R. *Descartes' Error: Emotion, Reason, and the Human Brain*. New York: Harper Perennial, 1994.

Dean, Tim. 'Portraits of a University.' *Traffic East Magazine* 12 (2007). <http://www.trafficeast.com/archives/issue-twelve/portraits-of-a-university>.

De Botton, Alain. 'A Meeting of Minds.' *The Telegraph* 7 April 2001. <http://www.telegraph.co.uk/culture/4722744/A-meeting-of-minds.html>.

Deleuze, Gilles, and Félix Guattari. *What Is Philosophy?* 1991. Trans. Hugh Tomlinson and Graham Burchell. New York: Columbia UP, 1994.

Didion, Joan. 'The Year of Hoping for Stage Magic.' *The New York Times* 4 March 2007. <http://www.nytimes.com/2007/03/04/theater/04didi.html?adxnnl=1&pagewanted=1&adxnnlx=1305745538–0IOei9F67JU7w6msjlh/YQ>.

————. *The Year of Magical Thinking*. New York: Alfred A. Knopf, 2005.

————. *The Year of Magical Thinking: The Play*. New York: Vintage, 2007.

Durrant, Nancy. 'Comedian David Hoyle Is No Drag.' *The Sunday Times* 21 April 2009. <http://entertainment.timesonline.co.uk/tol/arts_and_entertainment/stage/comedy/article6133256.ece>.

Eriksson, Stig A., and Mette Bøe Lyngstad. Interview with Augusto Boal about *Rainbow of Desire* – From Europe to South-America. 2004. <http://www.dramaiskolen.no/dramaiskolen/media/Interview%20with%20Augusto%20Boal2pdf.pdf>.

Evreinov, Nikolai. *The Theatre in Life*. Trans. and ed. Alexander I. Nazaroff. London: George G. Harrap, 1927.

Eyre, Richard. *National Service: Diary of a Decade at the National Theatre*. London: Bloomsbury, 2003.

Foucault, Michel. *The History of Sexuality: The Will to Knowledge*. 1976. *The History of Sexuality*. Vol. 1. Trans. Robert Hurley. New York: Vintage, 1990.

————. *The History of Sexuality: The Care of the Self*. 1984. *The History of Sexuality*. Vol. 3. Trans. Robert Hurley. New York: Vintage, 1988.

Freud, Sigmund. *Fragment of an Analysis of a Case of Hysteria*. 1901; 1905. *The Standard Edition of the Complete Psychological Works of Sigmund Freud*. Vol. 7 (1901–1905). Trans. James Strachey in collaboration with Anna Freud. London: Vintage, 2001. 7–134.

————. *The Interpretation of Dreams*. 1899–1900; 1955. Trans. and ed. James Strachey. New York: Basic Books, 2010.

————. *Jokes and Their Relation to the Unconscious*. 1905. *The Standard Edition of the Complete Psychological Works of Sigmund Freud*. Vol. 8 (1905). Trans. James Strachey in collaboration with Anna Freud. London: Vintage, 2001.

————. *Moses and Monotheism: An Outline of Psycho-Analysis and Other Works*. *The Standard Edition of the Complete Psychological Works of Sigmund Freud*. Vol. 23 (1937–1939). Trans. James Strachey in collaboration with Anna Freud London: Vintage, 2001.

————. 'Psychopathic Characters on the Stage.' 1905–1906; 1942. *The Standard Edition of the Complete Psychological Works of Sigmund Freud*.

Vol. 7 (1901–1905). Trans. James Strachey in collaboration with Anna Freud. London: Vintage, 2001. 305–10.

Furedi, Frank. *Therapy Culture: Cultivating Vulnerability in an Uncertain Age*. London: Routledge, 2004.

Grant, David. 'We Carried Your Secrets.' *Irish Theatre Magazine* 4 December 2010. <http://www.irishtheatremagazine.ie/Reviews/Current/We-Carried-Your-Secrets>.

Green, André. *The Tragic Effect: The Oedipus Complex in Tragedy*. Cambridge: Cambridge UP, 1979.

Hattenstone, Simon. 'In the Name of the Father' [interview with Daniel Day-Lewis]. *The Guardian* 28 February 2003. <http://www.guardian.co.uk/culture/2003/feb/28/artsfeatures.danieldaylewis>.

Heddon, Deirdre. 'Box Story.' *Bobby Baker: Redeeming Features of Daily Life*. Ed. Bobby Baker and Michèle Barrett. London: Routledge, 2007. 230–37.

Heddon, Deirdre, and Adrian Howells. 'From Talking to Silence: A Confessional Journey.' *PAJ: A Journal of Performance and Art* 33.1 (2011): 1–12.

Howells, Adrian. 'Being Adrienne ... ' Talk delivered as part of the CASCPP 'Artists Talking the Domestic' event, in conjunction with the AHRB Women's Writing for Performance Project and the Nuffield Theatre. 4 March 2005. <http://www.cascpp.lancs.ac.uk/documents/beingadrienne.pdf>.

————. University of Glasgow Research Page. <http://www.gla.ac.uk/departments/theatrefilmtelevisionstudies/ourstaff/howells/held/>.

Hurley, Erin. *Theatre & Feeling*. Basingstoke, UK: Palgrave Macmillan, 2010.

Jarry, Alfred. *Ubu Roi*. 1896. Trans. Barbara Wright. New York: New Directions, 1961.

Jennings, Sue. *Healthy Attachments and Neuro-Dramatic-Play*. London: Jessica Kingsley, 2011.

Johnson, Terry. *Hysteria: Or Fragments of an Analysis of an Obsessional Neurosis*. London: Methuen, 1993.

Jones, Phil. *Clinical Work and Research into Practice. Drama as Therapy*. Vol. 2. London: Routledge, 2010.

————. *Theory, Practice and Research*. 2nd ed. *Drama as Therapy*. Vol. 1. London: Routledge, 2007.

Kane, Sarah. *4.48 Psychosis*. 2000. *Sarah Kane: Complete Plays*. London: Methuen, 2001. 203–46.

Klein, Melanie. 'Early Analysis.' 1923. *Love, Guilt and Reparation, and Other Works 1921–1945*. London: Vintage, 1998.

Lacan, Jacques. 'Desire and the Interpretation of Desire in Hamlet.' 1959. *Literature and Psychoanalysis: The Question of Reading: Otherwise*. Ed. Shoshana Felman. Baltimore, MD: Johns Hopkins UP, 1977. 11–52.

———. *The Ethics of Psychoanalysis 1959–1960. The Seminar of Jacques Lacan*. Book 7. 1992. Trans. Dennis Porter. London: Routledge, 2008.

———. 'The Mirror Stage as Formative of the Function of the I as Revealed in Psychoanalytic Experience.' 1949. *Écrits: A Selection*. 1977. Trans. Alan Sheridan. London: Routledge, 2001.

Laing, R. D. *Knots*. New York: Penguin, 1971.

McConachie, Bruce. *Engaging Audiences: A Cognitive Approach to Spectating in the Theatre*. Basingstoke, UK: Palgrave Macmillan, 2008.

McPherson, Conor. *Four Plays*. London: Nick Hern, 1999.

———. *Shining City*. New York: Theatre Communications, 2005.

Moreno, Jacob Levy. *The Theatre of Spontaneity*. 1924. North-West Psychodrama Association, 2012.

Neilson, Anthony. *The Wonderful World of Dissocia*. London: Methuen Drama, 2007.

Phillips, Adam. *Equals*. New York: Basic Books, 2002.

———. *Houdini's Box: On the Arts of Escape*. London: Faber and Faber, 2001.

———. *On Flirtation*. Cambridge, MA: Harvard UP, 1996.

Pitches, Jonathan. *Science and the Stanislavsky Tradition of Acting*. London: Routledge, 2006.

Quinn, Gavin, ed. *One: Healing with Theatre*. Dublin: Lilliput, 2005.

Rees, Jasper. 'Ruby Wax: Losing It.' *The Telegraph* 6 April 2010. <http://www.telegraph.co.uk/culture/theatre/theatre-features/7560414/Ruby-Wax-Losing-It.html>

Roach, Joseph. *The Player's Passion: Studies in the Science of Acting*. Ann Arbor: U of Michigan P, 1993.

Stanislavski, Constantin. *An Actor Prepares*. 1937. Trans. Elizabeth Reynolds Hapgood. London: Routledge, 1980.

Strasberg, Lee. *A Dream of Passion: The Development of the Method*. 1987. Ed. Evangeline Morphos. New York: Plume, 1988.

Strindberg, August. *Inferno/From an Occult Diary*. London: Penguin, 1979.

————. *Miss Julie and Other Plays*. Trans. and ed. Michael Robinson. New York: Oxford UP, 1998.

————. *The Plays*. Vol. 1. Trans. Gregory Motton. London: Oberon, 2000.

————. *Strindberg's Letters*. Vol. 2 (1892–1912). Trans. and ed. Michael Robinson. London: U of Chicago P, 1992.

Vankin, Deborah. 'Laugh Factory to Add Therapy to Stand-up Comics' Routine.' *Los Angeles Times* 9 February 2011.

Watkins, Neil. 'The Year of Magical Wanking.' Unpublished manuscript. 2010.

Winnicott, D. W. 'The Capacity to Be Alone.' 1958. *The Maturational Processes and the Facilitating Environment*. London: Karnac, 2007. 29–36.

————. *Playing and Reality*. 1971. London: Routledge, 2005.

Wright, Nicholas. *Mrs Klein*. London: Nick Hern, 2010.

Zarrilli, Phillip B. *Psychophysical Acting: An Intercultural Approach after Stanislavski*. London: Routledge, 2008.

Zola, Émile. Extract from 'Naturalism in the Theatre.' 1881. Trans. Albert Bermel. *The Harcourt Brace Anthology of Drama*. 2nd ed. Ed. W. B. Worthen. New York: Harcourt Brace College Publishers, 1996. 761–67.

Select websites

The Sesame Institute: <http://www.sesame-institute.org/>.

Stand Up For Mental Health: <http://www.standupformentalhealth.com/>.

index

acknowledgements

I would like to thank series editors Jen Harvie and Dan Rebellato for commissioning this book, and Dan for seeing it through to publication, along with Jenni Burnell and Felicity Noble at Palgrave Macmillian. Thanks also to the anonymous readers for their advice. Colleagues and students at Trinity College Dublin, Queen Mary, University of London, and Birkbeck, University of London deserve a mention for engaging with this research in various ways and at different stages. I'm especially grateful to my one-time mentor at Trinity, Brian Singleton. I would like to acknowledge funding from the Irish Research Council for the Humanities and Social Sciences which, in part, supported the writing of this book. Love and thanks to Adam, Aileen, Brian, David, Fiona, Laurence and Phillip for their friendship during and beyond this project. And a special mention for Áine, to whom the book is dedicated.